I like *being old* . . .

I like the freedom and awareness I have. I like sometimes doing things that are outrageous. I like enjoying
those who are different from me, and I like knowing the
many things that I didn't know at thirty and forty and
fifty years of age.

My Croning began a time of reflection, acceptance,
and satisfaction—a time of new responsibilities, a time of
reveling in my being and my maturity.

To become a Crone, an elder, or just plain old is a passage from knowledge to wisdom.

I know that what is important in my life has changed,
and I revel in that fact. Old is a positive place for me to
be. And that is wisdom.

— *Ruth Gardner*
Author and Crone

About the Author

At sixty-six years of age, with a successful forty-two year marriage and two grown daughters under her belt, Ruth Gardner has earned the title of Crone. Her involved dedication to women's issues dates back to 1976, when she, along with several other women, was lauded in *Ms.* and other women's periodicals for production of the *Women's Network Directory*, a Minnesota publication. In the past ten years, Ruth has co-organized the Tucson group Desert Crones, assisted in developing and producing the video *Celebration of Age* (see bibliography), and has been an active teacher in the field of Wise Women for University of Arizona extension classes. Ruth has been interviewed for numerous printed and visual media, including an appearance on the video *Grandmothers Speak, Healing the Earth* (see bibliography).

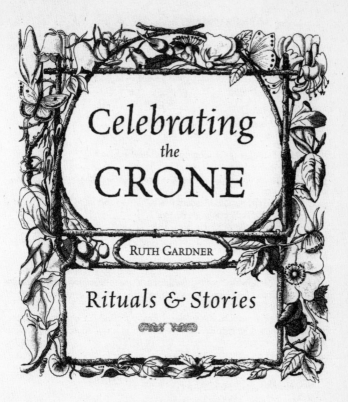

Celebrating
the
CRONE

Ruth Gardner

Rituals & Stories

1999
Llewellyn Publications
St. Paul, Minnesota 55164-0383
U.S.A.

FIRST EDITION
First Printing, 1999

Cover design by Lisa Novak
Editing and book design by Kjersti Monson
Interior illustrations by Carrie Westfall

Library of Congress Cataloging-in-Publication Data
Gardner, Ruth, 1933–
    Celebrating the crone: rituals & stories / Ruth Gardner. —1st ed.
         p.   cm.
    Includes bibliographical references (p.   ) and index.
    ISBN 1-56718-292-5 (trade paper)
    1. Crones—religious life   I. Title.
BL625.7.G355   1999
305.4—dc21   99-32678
                                           CIP

Llewellyn Worldwide does not participate in, endorse, or have any authority or responsibility concerning private business transactions between our authors and the public.
    All mail addressed to the author is forwarded but the publisher cannot, unless specifically instructed by the author, give out an address or phone number.

Llewellyn Publications
A Division of Llewellyn Worldwide
P.O. Box 64383, Dept. K292-5
St. Paul, MN 55164-0383 U.S.A.
www.llewellyn.com

To Write to the Author

If you wish to contact the author or would like more information about this book, please write to the author in care of Llewellyn Worldwide, and we will forward your request. Both the author and publisher appreciate hearing from you and learning of your enjoyment of this book and how it has helped you. Llewellyn Worldwide cannot guarantee that every letter written to the author will be answered, but all will be forwarded. Please write to:

Ruth Gardner
c/o Llewellyn Worldwide
P.O. Box 64383, Dept. K292-5
St. Paul, MN 55164-0383 U.S.A.

Please enclose a self-addressed stamped envelope for reply, or $1.00 to cover costs. If outside the U.S.A., enclose international postal reply coupon.

For Llewellyn's free full-color catalog, write to *New Worlds* at the above address or call 1-800-THE-MOON.

Dedicated to Ron...

. . . without whom this book may never have been finished. He was my inspiration, my friend, my supporter, my lover, and my husband for forty-two years. He daily shared his life with me, giving me experiences that were warm, exciting, satisfying, challenging, and productive.

Contents

Contents

Foreword
by Patricia Monaghan

When we are children, we are told stories of ugly witches living in the woods whose sole purpose is to steal children like Hansel and Gretel—terrifying women who should be avoided at all costs.

If fairy tales paint a scary image of older women, the electronic babysitter is worse. On television, we rarely see images of older women at all. When we do, they are helpless victims who fall and can't get up, psychopathic landladies, frightened victims, or (very occasionally) a queen or similarly distant figure.

Is it any wonder that we grow up fearful of the Crone?

Deep in our minds, we may store memories of the warm lap of a loving grandmother, or of the wild enthusiastic power of an aunt. However, as our families live more geographically distant from elders, many children grow up without a memorable counter-image to the negative stereotyping of the Crone which children's tales and media provide.

Meanwhile, cosmetic surgery is a booming business with much tucking and nipping devoted to removing signs of age from women's faces. The emotional history written in laugh lines around a woman's eyes or worry lines between her eyebrows is erased, as though the alphabet of deep experience and deeper feelings is not worthy of being read.

Ironically, an antidote to the negative propaganda against aging women can be found in one of its sources: fairy tales wherein the wicked witch appears. In Hansel and Gretel, Rapunzel, Snow White, and similar childhood stories, we encounter the power of a primal goddess whose people, forced to convert to another religion, nonetheless held on to her image as the world around them changed—the "witches" of fairy tales are the ancient Crone goddesses of their people. They survived for countless generations by being declared "just a figure in a children's story." Hidden in plain sight,

Crones avoided coming under the thumb of a religion that had no place for the primal power of aged women.

This has happened over and over in human history. A people whose mythology included a Crone figure were invaded or otherwise forced to convert to a new religion—but mothers still told children the old tales on winter evenings as they gathered near the hearth. Such children's tales are a rich treasury of subjugated mythologies, sometimes including material that is thousands of years old, now told by people who have no clue about its original meaning.

Sometimes the Crone survived in an even stranger way—by becoming a figure of terror kept alive by the very culture that overthrew her. Such demonization was the fate of Lamia the Canaanite (considered a bogey-woman by the Hebrews) and Medusa the Anatolian (given snakes for hair by the Greeks). Originally powerful and complex goddesses, they were diminished to simplistic monsters—but nonetheless survived.

In fairy tales, however, the Crone is not demonized; she is simply caricatured—her power made to seem silly, her needs petulant. Such is the case with Mother Gothel, the Crone who refuses to let Rapunzel's father steal rampion (a kind of onion) from her flourishing garden. Here we have a typical transformation of the Crone goddess. Her image remains: an older woman whose power of fertility has left the limitations of her physical being and diffused into the world around her. Witness her garden, a splendidly thriving place, which attracts the envy of Rapunzel's mother.

The story is usually told as though Dame Gothel envies the pregnant woman, yet the story starts when Rapunzel's mother becomes consumed with desire for what Dame Gothel has. The old woman's fertility is no longer confined to her womb. She is a vast power of fertility, surrounded by a garden of phenomenal proportions—a kind of fairy tale Findhorn.

Thus, it's not just rampion the pregnant woman desires, it's Dame Gothel's power. In mythology, gardens often represent feminine sexuality, so it's curious that the pregnant woman compulsively urges her husband to invade Dame Gothel's garden. The sexual power of

the Crone draws all to her, even those who do not recognize what they are experiencing.

The woman is not, however, content with a taste of
the rampion, and sends her husband back many times
to steal the power of the Crone. Finally Dame Gothel
captures him. She has enough to share, and may have
done so had she been asked, but she was not. Dame
Gothel is outraged by the theft. She demands payment
in the form of the child the couple is expecting.

In fairy tales, we often find Crone figures linked
with young women: Baba Yaga and Vasillisa the Fair,
Gretel and the witch, Little Red Riding Hood and her
granny. The nubile, prepubescent girl has much in
common with the post-menopausal witch, and not
only because one is not yet physically fertile while the
other has passed beyond that stage. There is a wild
freedom about the feminine force in a body that is not
using a portion of its energy on the reproductive cycle.
Thus, when Rapunzel comes to Dame Gothel, it is a
joining of two similar forces.

Dame Gothel puts Rapunzel in a tower, a building whose phallic imagery is continually remarked upon by commentators of the tale. The implication of such arm-chair Freudians is that the Crone, being without the ability to physically reproduce, has thus become some-how masculated (this word does not exist as an oppo-site to emasculate, though it should). Dame Gothel, by this reasoning, has become somehow the opposite of feminine simply because she no longer bears children. The Crone is no longer a woman, because woman is defined by her fertility.

Yet these commentators are far from consistent in their imagery, for maidens are not usually confined in the tip of phalluses. And what could Rapunzel's hair, streaming out of the tower, conceivably represent in this framework? As for the prince climbing the tower—well, as girls today like to say, don't go there.

Freud himself pointed out that a cigar is sometimes just a cigar. Finding phallic imagery in every erect object may lead us to wrong assumptions about meaning. It is

instructive that the tale of Rapunzel is so often interpreted in this fashion, however—it reveals some of the
biases against Crones as they appear in fairy tales.

Assume, by contrast, that the Crone is not the evil
figure in this story, but is instead a figure of transformation. Rapunzel's mother intuits this, which is why she so
craves the power of the Crone's garden. When Dame
Gothel is given the girl, she elevates her. If one looks at
the tower as a representative of the human body—and
buildings in dreams are often female bodies—then
Dame Gothel puts Rapunzel in touch with her mind,
placing her as she does at the top of the building.

Hair in dreams and myths often represents thought.
Thus, under the Crone's guidance, Rapunzel's thoughts
grow strong and long enough to form a ladder for
Dame Gothel. Working together, the girl and the Crone
have built an imaginative space for themselves. This, in
fact, happens frequently when young girls and Crones
spend time together—a marvelous, playful, creative
space is made in this world.

Eventually the prince must come. When the girl reaches her reproductive years, she and the Crone must bid farewell. Another girl will doubtless come to learn with Dame Gothel, but for Rapunzel there will be many years ahead before she encounters the Crone again—this time in herself.

This is a very different reading of the fairy tale that is usually offered—one which begins with the presumption that Dame Gothel is a positive rather than negative force in the story. Looking at the Crones of myth and fairy tale in this way, we can find many treasures yet to be unearthed, much human wisdom encoded and waiting to be revealed. As women in their Croning years reevaluate these images in light of the power and energy they feel within themselves, we are likely to see many new and exciting visions of the Crone revealed.

Acknowledgments

To all the women who have gone before me, to all of those interested in Croning, and to the many who have encouraged me by offering their experiences, thoughts, reflections, memories, and inspirations, I give thanks.

I am grateful in particular to Connie Spittler, Lois Lockhart, Grace Eggert, Marlene Thompson, Hannah Blue Heron, Joni Troutner, Sue Alexander and Caitlin Williams—all fellow Desert Crones (see page 188) who kept inspiring me not only with their words for publication but their unceasing creativity. I am also grateful to Crones Nell Robie, Margaret Cubberly, Joan Weiss Hollenbeck and Pat Watkins, who first offered their Croning ceremonies for publication in *Crone Chronicles* (see page 198) and then this book. I cannot forget Shekhinah Mountainwater, Carol Laughing Water, Dawn Mills, and Antiga, who have allowed me the privilege of reprinting their beautiful words in this book. To Sarah Dagg, who hesitated and then came forth to offer me so much, many thanks. In addition to the their special contributions, these women also cheerfully allowed me to interview them for material used throughout the book.

To all of the other women writers and musicians who cheerfully allowed me to use parts of their works, I give thanks.

I am forever grateful to my daughter, Renee Gardner. She supported me with her talent, presence, and approval through my entrance into Cronehood. Also thanks to my second daughter, Robin, who has always supported me with her love and acceptance.

Most importantly, thanks to my mate, Ron, who helped me with editing—over and over again—and cooked wonderful inspirational meals for us while I sat at the computer. He died shortly after the book was finished. To Shirley Fritchoff who helped me with editing after Ron died, I give great thanks.

Introduction

On a warm, tranquil evening in Tucson, Arizona, a group of old women met at a quiet shaded park. Ancient women's songs came softly from a guitar and the lips of a skilled musician as the group assembled. Some brilliantly dressed Crones purified each woman with sage, called the directions, and opened the circle. The purple altar cloth held salt, water, earth, flowers, a raven wing, burning candles, and various mementos and pictures arranged by those involved.

An exercise allowed participants to share memories of accomplishments, sadness, and success. One Crone welcomed the Women-Being-Croned to the Sisterhood of Crones, another sprinkled salt at their feet, and a third sang to them as she draped a purple braid of many shades over the shoulder of each. A final Crone read a group Intention-for-the-Future. With the closing of the circle, the formal ceremony ended.

As the music began again, Crones sang and danced where the circle had been while others set out food for the feast to come.

The festivities quieted as a white-shirted gray-haired man approached some of the celebrants and asked who was in charge. When directed to the facilitator, he showed his County Sheriff badge and demanded to know what was going on. He subsequently informed the Crones that, without a permit, they must disperse immediately.

The officer continued, explaining that his office had received a call requesting that he "break up a group of witches in the park."

After a little congenial conversation and an explanation of the purpose of our gathering, the lack of a permit was apologized for. The badged one agreed to allow the Crones twenty minutes to pack up the now fully laden tables, and then left the still joyful women to the park.

A different kind of aging ceremony—"jubilees"—are celebrated in many churches in various religious orders. In a jubilee, the honored one tells her life story, her history and experience, and is honored by others' memories of her religious life. In the past she was crowned with a wreath of flowers, but corsages are now the norm. A formal religious ceremony is conducted including music, a mass, and scripture readings. The celebrant's works are exhibited, described, and acclaimed. The ceremony is an acknowledgment by the community of a woman's passage into a new phase of life. It recognizes her changing role from active to reflective as she prepares for the final greatest celebration. *This* form of celebration is accepted by most who hear about it or are privileged to attend.

Are these two kinds of celebrations really so different from each other? Why are the participants in the park ceremony "busted" while the church ceremony is accepted by the majority of society? Both ceremonies celebrate the entrance into a new chronological age, both ceremonies celebrate by use of ritual, both ceremonies have more in common than not. Who legislates what is acceptable and what is not?

The general lack of acceptance of old women in our society frustrates and amazes me. Several of the women I interviewed for this book told me they were afraid to share their interest or involvement in Croning with their families. "I didn't think they would understand. I was afraid they would belittle me or try to stop me," one of them said. If age is disguised by plastic surgery, dye jobs, or falsehoods, can it be avoided? Isn't it easier to accept and enjoy rather than deny and struggle?

When I decided to celebrate reaching "old age" I searched vainly for appropriate resources. All the while, other women repeatedly told me that at sixty I wasn't old. Libraries had little to offer on the subject. Despite the discouragement, there were wonderful circles of women willing to risk and care, to be honest about their age and also about what they had to offer the world. With their help, I did have a wonderful, memorable, spiritual ceremony. I eventually decided to interview modern Crones and research and develop a written record for those interested in celebrating this stage of life.

This information is not directed to women of any particular religion. It is directed to any woman for whom it has meaning. During the process of my interviews, many women spoke of their spirituality rather than their religion. Croning for me was a very spiritual experience and totally separate from any established religion.

The
Beginning

PART I

There was a time when the earth was considered female and received universal worship because she was the universal parent; a time when most people believed that all living things, including people and animals, emerged from the earth. There was a time when philosophers believed the Earth Mother was the mysterious power that woke everything to life; when women were the healers who were respected and sought out for healing and advice. There was a time when *Crone* meant "crown" and a Crone was called Wise Woman, when *hag* meant "holy one," when *saga* meant "female sage," and when elders were venerated and respected.

Old and *Crone* are not synonymous, but in our culture they have many of the same connotations. The title *Crone* hasn't always been derogatory. Two thousand years ago, very old women were particularly important members of communities. They were leaders, counselors, and healers. They were the fulfillment of female experience and wisdom. Young women moved from the excited and unconstrained youthfulness of the Maiden through the life-sustaining position of the Mother (biological or metaphoric) to the loving, mature, and confident wisdom and understanding of the Crone. As women aged, they used their experience and memories to benefit the community. Age was seen as a time of arriving, of reaching the pinnacle when those elders could share their wisdom. Old was not good or bad—it was a measurement without judgment. The word *Crone* was not good or bad—it was just the title of a special stage in women's lives. Crones were considered the wise and learned of the community.

The Goddess Survivor

The recognition of women as positive respected beings has changed. Not suddenly, but gradually—as is the case with many changes of loss. In many minds today, *Crone* is synonymous with wrinkled, dependent, frail, debilitated, ugly, grotesque, dispensable, useless, or unimportant old woman. That false belief is a result of the events that formed it. The burning of women, the persecution of women, and the degradation of women as chattel are

4

all a part of history and still affect us today. Generations passed and little girls were taught by clergy and their fathers that they were *lesser*. Mothers knew that teaching their daughters to deny themselves meant survival—so they taught them denial and acceptance. We became so used to denying ourselves that perhaps, despite changing laws, we still find it difficult to claim our rightful places. But now:

> *There is a grassroots women's spirituality movement that is worldwide yet unorganized: women are gathering together in a small group or are acting individually, observing seasons and important transitions, doing rituals, making altars, finding symbols that express important spiritual and psychological themes and feelings. There is very little tradition to follow, and so women follow intuition and do what feels spontaneously right. After four to six thousand years of patriarchy and patriarchal gods, in the passing of spiritual traditions in a mother-line from mother to daughter, awareness of priestesses, healers, wise women, female divinity, or a Mother Goddess is lost from memory. In the spontaneous arising of a woman's*

spirituality movement, however, "re-membering" may be occurring. In sacred places, where the Goddess once was worshiped or venerated, women enact rituals. In circles, women celebrate the seasons. Might it be that women are resonating with a morphic field as they bring the Goddess back into human consciousness? Might contemporary ritual reflect what has gone on before and is adding to it?[1]

5

This statement by Jean Shinoda Bolen articulates very clearly some of what is beginning to happen to us now. Croning ceremonies counter the resistance to aging that is so prevalent in our Western culture. Women meet together to celebrate their age and fully experience it, recognizing in the process that the presence of others supports who they are and encourages them to find joy and comfort in that. Many women experience immense growth as a result of their ceremony—processing with other Crones, learning how much they can grow by accepting and loving who they are, and learning how much can come to them through sharing.

The Wisdom of Reclamation

6
Women have told me that they feel guilty being Croned (knowing that Crone means wisdom) when they don't feel wise. Most of us have been taught that we cannot claim wisdom without demonstrating someone else's idea of wisdom. So what *is* Crone wisdom? Where does it come from? What makes one wise?

Crone wisdom is a mysterious quality some like to call *women's intuition*—which avoids calling it what it really is: intelligence, experience, and trust in one's innate ability to know. Most folks agree that wisdom develops over time from experience. Women are schooled in being responsible for lives other than their own. In order to assume this responsibility, we must be quick learners and acute observers.

Wise Women are often described as having finely developed skills in logic, reason, and perceptiveness. As we accumulate that experience, we display better judgment and skill in our ability to learn from mistakes. It seems to me that anyone who survives to her Crone years

has acquired wisdom just because she *has* survived.
Characteristics of Wise Women include the ability to:

- Learn from past mistakes
- Admit errors (a hallmark of wisdom)
- Be practical (a skill that helps solve problems)
- Be empathetic, understanding, and caring
- Use knowledge and experience to help others
- Trust your own instincts and hunches
- Avoid seeking strictly *right* or *wrong* answers
- Tolerate ambiguity as life knowledge expands
- Manage your own life effectively
- Create harmony with those around you
- Accept challenges to your views and use them to examine opposing points of view
- Enjoy satisfaction gained from helping others
- Accept the feelings that accompany experience

Choosing the name "Crone" is a deliberate act by women to undermine the biased belief system that is so prevalent in our culture. That system devalues old women by ignoring the experience, knowledge, and wisdom that they have acquired through living. By bringing the term *Crone* into common usage, women survivors defy those who disparage them. Crones champion their right to be recognized as contributing members of society, as strong and valuable resources entitled to respect. With full awareness of the word's current negative connotations, women choose it to confront the issues facing aging women. They choose it to raise important questions about attitudes and feelings toward those issues, and to bring those concepts into the light where values can be revealed and strengths acknowledged. From the insights gained through their efforts, we can all learn to honor women's experience.

Women have many reasons for deciding to formally announce their passage. Many women whom I interviewed spoke of their need to overcome the traditional negative associations ascribed to old women—and to the word *Crone*.

Wise Women, On Croning...

Passages in life require some kind of ceremony.
Reading about the experience of other women in
Crone Chronicles gave me the inspiration to stage a
ritual of my own when I reached sixty-five.

—A WISE WOMAN

[My ritual] was a way of declaring publicly that I
am a Crone and proud of it—a personal embracing
of my age and being. It was a recognition that death
is just around the corner and although I prepare
for it, I don't fear it.

—PROUD TO BE CRONED

Croning is a part of my physical, intellectual,
and spiritual path.

—A CRONE THROUGHOUT

Cronehood is the last phase of my life circle
which will end with my death and my leaving this

realm. Having a ritual was my way of
accepting . . . all of the above.

—AN OLD WOMAN

I belong to a woman's group at my church who
perform various rituals. A friend and I were invited
to be ceremonially Croned . . . when we were sixty-
five years old. I wanted to affirm *me* as I am, to
make a statement to friends, relatives, and society
that older women are visible—they are to be lis-
tened to and reckoned with. We have much
to offer. Do not ignore us.

—CRONED WITH A FRIEND

My decision to go through with the ritual brought to
my attention my avoidance of talking about age and
aging. It is a natural sequence in life, and I am in this
twilight time. I've learned to accept that other[s] are
seeing me differently than I may be feeling myself.

—A WHITE-HAIRED BEAUTY

I had never heard of a Crone ritual until women in a Wise Women drumming group I belonged to started talking about it. Originally the word *Crone* antagonized me. I thought, "That's not me. I'm not a Crone. Crones are ugly, old, useless women." But I thought I ought to know more about Crones—about who and what they are. I discovered it meant recognition of my status of age—a ceremony to honor that. I felt good thinking about it. It was an outward proclamation of my change of status in the world.

—A SOUTHWESTERN CRONE

I have been involved in teaching workshops for women, especially old women, for quite a few years and use the word *Crone* frequently yet I had never heard of having a ritual to announce the entrance into Cronehood. I first heard of it when I became involved in Desert Crones in Tucson. To me, *Crone* means a strong old woman. A ceremony or ritual just publicly declares that fact.

—UNDERSTANDING CRONE

I was fiercely determined not to be depressed and
defeated by turning sixty-five. I refused to accept
the idea that I was finished when I thought I was an
interesting, vital woman. I wanted to recognize this
new stage of my life by calling my friends and
daughter together to acknowledge me as a Crone.
I even took a new name, "Cailleach"—a Celtic goddess, to symbolize . . . [my] transition into a Crone.

—A Vibrant Crone

I originally found the term very unacceptable. It
meant all that I thought wrong with a woman. I don't
think I even identified that it was a woman of age but
that it was a bad, unsuitable word used to put women
down. As I struggled with my inflexible self, I learned
that many old women who discovered the strength
that comes with knowing who they are were calling
themselves Crones. They had freed themselves from
being something for someone else; freed themselves
to see one another just the way they were, not the
way others might want them to be. I learned they
share feelings, fears, and insights, accept each other's
changes, and encourage each other's growth. They

appreciate that "old" is not a bad word; that it is not a statement of decline but one of time.

—VIBRANT CRONE, CONTINUED

Driving through the White Mountains
in a snow storm after spending nearly
a week with a friend on the Hopi reservation,
I reflected on [my friend's] introduction to carving
as a meditation practice. We had carved many symbols of women, goddesses, and aging. I dreamed of
[incorporating] a similar experience into a private
Croning ceremony. I believe when a woman
becomes old enough to be called *Crone,* it indicates
a time in her life when she can draw on her experiences to make decisions and to counsel others. I
wanted to experience the ceremony to introduce
myself into the time of the Wise Woman.
Anticipation of the ceremony forced me to look
forward into my life and consciously move into a
maturation plan for growth and commitment.

—AN ADVENTURESOME ARIZONAN

Croning is best done individually as a time to celebrate one woman's life and transition. Group Cronings can be wonderful but for such a special occasion it is important that there is time for each honored to tell her story; to listen to others tell their stories of her. It is a time to acknowledge the gift of one's life, the moving into the 'keeper' phase. To me the 'keeper' phase is the time when the Crone begins to share all that she has been storing within her with others. Sometimes it may be heirlooms or jewelry, but [it is] most assuredly the memories of her life— stories that her children can hear from no one else. Cronings should be done in churches, in kitchens, in gardens, with family and friends . . . sharing, giving, receiving, remembering, and honoring.

—A Religious Crone

Some Crones are reluctant to invite family members to participate in their ritual due to concerns that they won't understand:

> Unfortunately, I do feel . . . that I'm not free enough to share with my family my Croning because of my vision of their conservative views. I have written about it and put it away . . . so after I'm gone my family can read about it.
>
> —A CONCERNED ELDER

I invited my family to celebrate my birthday and I planned it all. I didn't use the word "Crone" and I didn't name the elements of the day the way I would have wished to. My family all came, partici-pated, enjoyed the storytelling, the sharing, and the receiving, and they enjoyed the food. They enjoyed all that they saw and I privately substituted words appealing to me after they were gone. It was a won-derful day. They mean well, it just takes them longer than some to understand anything that is different. I became aware of the fact I don't feel free

enough to share with my family my activity
because of my perception that their views are too
conservative for them to accept [my practices].

—A CRONE WITH HER OWN SOLUTION

Women who undergo this glorious, life-changing ceremony come from all kinds of religious backgrounds.
Most of them said they did not have to reconcile their
new status and methods of celebrating it with any prior
religious commitments . . .

I'm an atheist so there was no conflict.
I was a cradle Catholic who left the church in
my twenties with no regrets. Patriarchal religion
left a very bad taste in my mouth . . . although
thinking about it, my use of Indian prayer robes
and sweet grass *does* have something in common
with priestly vestments and palm leaves . . . .
Maybe there is no difference!

—A THOUGHTFUL CRONE

I tend toward Buddhism. I was unchurched as a child but my parents had Christian backgrounds. As a child, I actively searched for religious connections. I don't think the path matters. Croning was a very spiritual experience and had nothing to do with religion.

—ONE RECENTLY CRONED

I was raised as a Christian, but not very strict[ly]. In my forties I became dissatisfied with religion and in my middle fifties I heard about Wicca. I realized this is the way I lived my life anyway so [I] didn't change anything but the outward recognition. Croning is an adjunct to any route to which one applies herself.

—A COMMUNITY LEADER

Today I am a loose Christian who acknowledges the Pagan roots of Christianity. Yet I choose an entirely different path than most of my sisters . . .
How fortunate!

—QUICK-WITTED CRONE

Several years ago I wrote a letter of resignation
to the church into which I had been born and
raised. After three years of study, I realized that
I had to move away from the patriarchy of that
philosophy in order to mature into an
understanding of the sacred feminine.

—A DARK-HAIRED CRONE

Nun's jubilees—their celebrations of years in the
religious order—are wonderful, joyful, spiritual
times in a nun's life. The pattern of them follows
the Croning rituals in very many ways. They are
done to celebrate a woman's life and transition.
People important to her are invited and there is celebration of her story. Her works are shown, music
and scripture are [included] and most of all, there
is acknowledgment or recognition for gifts given.
Croning rituals need to be done in churches and
anywhere else a Crone wants to celebrate.

—ROMAN CATHOLIC NUN

It's Good to Be Old

I too was exposed to my own defeating beliefs about the word *old*. I became aware of the obvious though often ignored testimony to ageism through my use of the word. I had accepted *Crone* as having a very positive meaning but I avoided calling myself or others old. *Older, elder,* or *senior* are words I used in order to avoid saying *old*.

I finally realized that being old has nothing to do with feeling sick or well, tired or energetic, happy or unhappy, rejected or free, competent or knowledgeable. It has only to do with chronological age. One of the ways our society perpetuates ageism is by pretending that it doesn't exist. I've thought about the difference between being called "young lady," which I see as a compliment, and "old lady," which I know is an insult. The way I and most others in our society think about such matters is subtle, but those ways have unbelievable power. If I call any of my friends old, I want them to take it as a recognition that they have lived many years.

I *like* being old. I like the freedom and the awareness I have. I like not having to perform, not doing the sorts of things I used to do to be accepted. I like sometimes doing things that are outrageous. I like enjoying those who are different from me and I like knowing the many things that I didn't know at thirty and forty and fifty years of age. I like not having to go through all of the difficult learning experiences again that have made me the person I am today. I like celebrating having survived, not having to go back and suffer through so much in my past. I am proud to glory in the wonder of being old. My Croning began a time of reflection, acceptance, and satisfaction—a time of new responsibilities, a time of reveling in my being and my maturity. To become a Crone, an elder, or just plain old is a passage from knowledge to wisdom.

I know that a lot of what used to waste energy and cause worry in my life no longer matters. I know a lot of things that my children value and want to know. I know that what is important in my life has changed, and I revel in that fact. Old is a positive place for me to be. And that is wisdom.

The
Spirit Within

PART II

24

Many of the women interviewed for this book talked about the recognition of their power, their wisdom, and their ability to love themselves—often as a recent occurrence connected with their Croning ritual. Their acceptance of these qualities in themselves was not always spoken, but their acknowledgment of such attributes often ran deep throughout our conversations. It was easy to determine that they were all talking about recognizing the Goddess within. Since most of us have been conditioned to believe that the Higher Power, Holy Spirit, God—or whatever name fits for each individual—is *male,* it is sometimes difficult to remember that there is really no gender to the spirit.

What would life have been like for each of us if we could have imagined a wonderful, warm, nurturing Goddess Mother sheltering, protecting, and guiding us as little girls? What would it be like if we could see that perfect spirit within each of us as a warrior woman when the need arose? As a wise decisive female if what was needed was wise decisiveness? What would it be like if we saw a *feminine* god living within our beings?

Maybe that feminine god could be called the Goddess in all Her shapes and forms. Maybe we could then recognize and identify with that perfect part within us that has always been there. Perhaps She wouldn't even have to be called by the feminine gender but rather be a genderless spirit with whom we would identify and feel no fear.

Looking back in history, there was a time when all looked to feminine images for hope and help. Female deity images date as far back as any knowledge. They were called Goddess, Earth Mother, or Great Mother. Many writers describe a balanced (nonpatriarchal and nonmatriarchal) social system in Old Europe. One of the most interesting facts about Goddess-centered art is its lack of articles of war and male domination. There is instead a cooperative and more balanced focus.

Worship of the Earth Mother has probably been present since the time when people needed to assign a name to the deity that furnished their food. European-based and many other languages depict the earth as feminine. Just as the earth sprouted new life each spring, women gave birth to new life. The divine feminine is present in cave drawings, stone shapes, and sculptures that reach far back in history. She is sometimes pregnant; sometimes with large belly, breasts, and buttocks denoting fertility; sometimes a bird; and sometimes simply a graceful woman.

In Old Europe, the color black was associated with the earth—with fertility. The Crone's color is black (or purple), perhaps denoting her approaching return to the earth. It was a favorable color, used frequently in ritual. Associating the color with negativity is a relatively recent occurrence.

The Earth Mother has remained with humankind in one form or another for centuries. From Her presence as fertile earth to goddess to saint, even to the Virgin Mary, she has always been with us. She was and is eternal. She lives beyond time and space. She is with each one of us. The term *triple goddess* embraces the three stages of a woman's life. Her female triune manifests within us as Maiden, Mother, and Crone—each is a part of the whole. Although we may now be called Crone, we *are* still Maiden and Mother.

The Crone in Myth...

28

Through the years, the Crone has been called by many names. In the following pages, I have listed a few of her manifestations that are favorites of mine. All of these (and others) reside within each of us.

Athena

The original Athena may have come from Africa. In Libya, She was probably called Neith or Anath. Some consider Her a goddess of household industry; some believe She is a goddess of the working world. She is said to have invented the wheel, weaving, and sewer systems, and is strongly associated with peace. When we are in need of an inventive streak, She may be the goddess aspect that responds.

Brigid

This name was derived by the Celtic Irish. The name became Bridget in Christian Ireland. As a triple goddess in ancient Ireland, She was a goddess of smithcraft, of poetry and inspiration, and of healing and medicine.

She was also the symbol of fire. The Celts continued to worship their goddess even after Christianity came— instead of *goddess*, they called Her a saint. She may be the part of us we call upon when we need to express ourselves through poetry.

Demeter

According to Greek myth, Demeter was a triad: the winter earth mother, the hibernating seed Who was Her own daughter (Persephone), and the aged Crone (Hecate). Demeter is also another form of Gaia. She symbolized food-providing plants and natural produc- tion. She may be the grower of food that resides in us.

Diana

To the Romans, as ruler of the sun, moon, and earth, Diana made up a trinity. Another Diana triune included Egeria the water nymph and Virbius of the woodlands. To the Greeks She was Artemis, the warrior, the huntress of the night.[2] In Ephesus, the church tried to stop the worship of Her by consecrating the Temple of Artemis to "Our Lady." The bishop was astounded when crowds demanded "Our Artemis." Artemis is the warrior within Whom we can call upon when necessary.

Gaia

Greeks believed that in the beginning there was only dark, only chaos. Then the dark chaos became earth, the Great Mother, the oldest of divinities. The chaos became Gaia. She is the earth and the mother quality in each woman brought into being.

Inanna

Inanna was the source of earth's life blood, a goddess of procreation. Babylonians called Her Ishtar and believed that She descended into the underworld each year but always returned. She was also Nanna, Whom Christians called "God's grandmother." The Sumerians also called Her Queen of the Land. There is a story about Inanna having Her insensitive and ungrateful spouse carried off to the underworld. Later She repented and allowed him to return to the earth from time to time. Inanna could be the part of us that repents and corrects unloving behavior.

Isis

It has been said that Isis is the oldest of the old, that She has *always been*. Egyptians said She and Her twin were the creating and destroying goddesses: Mother of Life and Crone of Death. Her original name in Egypt was Au Set, but the Greeks changed Her name to Isis. She is often pictured with very large wings and was said to be the moon. The moon goddess is also a goddess of transitions and of healing. Isis was called the Lady of Ten Thousand Names. Perhaps Isis is the healer in us.

Kuan Yin

This Asian goddess is the most powerful goddess in all of the Orient. Among other things, She is a goddess of compassion, protector of children, guardian of the temple. When there is a need for compassion, Kuan Yin is the part of us that surfaces.

Persephone

Persephone, as She was known to the Greeks, was also known as Kore, as Hecate, and as ruler of the underworld. She was a death goddess. Persephone of the underworld was part of a triune that included Demeter of the earth and Hecate of the moon, Who lived in the sky. There are many variations on how Persephone became the underworld goddess, one of which describes Her living above ground and being abducted by Hades. Thereafter, She could spend only brief periods of time on earth—and when She did, Demeter made the earth bloom. In Her underworld guise, She may be the dark side in each of us.

Venus

Venus, the goddess of love, is also known as Freya or Aphrodite. In the context of Venus, love refers to sexual love as well as love of beauty and tenderness. Venus was said to have been born of the sea. She is the part of us that needs to give love.

The Goddess: All-That-Is

The Holy Spirit—the Goddess—is the All-That-Is in each of us. No matter what She is called or what part of Her we need, She is there and within us always. Regardless of whether Her spirit is referred to by gender or not, She is present. And we can call on Her anytime, for She is us.

Countless images have been retrieved from the earth, some of which have rested there for many thousands of years. These images remind us that we all are part of the All-That-Is. Whatever She is called and wherever She rests, She is a representation of Nature.

She is All-That-Is. We are one.[3]

Designing a Ritual

PART III

Ritual is the oldest and most successful method of experiencing truth in a deeply meaningful way. Too often ritual is seen as superstitious and somehow anti-spiritual. Some religious leaders and many nonreligious people deny the power and personal satisfaction that can be invoked with a formal and personal circle ritual.

Usually the most important aspect of any ritual is its purpose. The purpose may be to seek strength for the present or the future, improve relations with the divine, deepen spiritual understanding, or all of the above.

In order to plan your ritual, you need to determine the following: What do you need? What do you want? Who or what spiritual deities are important to you? How do you want to use your favorite colors? The real power of any ritual comes from what you bring to it.

Defining the Crone

The noun *Crone* means woman who is wise, elder. It implies ancient female wisdom. The Crone is a sacred archetype living in each woman. The verb *to Crone* means to enact a ritual announcing that the subject has learned to integrate her many years' seasoning into wisdom and compassion and to express her fullness for the good of all. In ancient times, *Crone* meant "to crown." In modern German, *krone* means "crown."

The Croning Ritual

Croning is a formal ritual about accepting the passage from knowledge to wisdom and recognizing that wisdom comes from experience. It is an announcement of passage, a celebration of the power, passion, and purpose of ancient female wisdom.

Who Should Participate?

Croning can be done individually, in groups of only women, in groups of family members, in groups of friends, or in any way the Cronee wants it to happen. Some women celebrate alone. Others plan a picnic or a formal dinner. Some celebrants share the experience with other women in a formal circle, and many choose to have their honored friends and relatives present. Sometimes men are included. Sometimes not.

When Will I Be Ready?

I was unable to find any consistent age when such ceremonies have traditionally occurred. Some celebrate when the woman felt ready to celebrate, others enjoy this solemn ritual at menopause. I have found some evidence that a common time (astrologically) is after an old woman's second Saturn return, which occurs around the age of fifty-six to fifty-eight. The most important part of deciding to have a personal Croning is being ready. When the Crone is ready, it's time for the ceremony.

The three stages of a woman's life—Maiden, Mother and Crone—all deserve to be celebrated.

The Maiden. This first stage symbolizes the pure sweet girl, and is often associated with the color white. This time before menses is the time of innocence. Various cultures celebrate leaving that stage of innocence and entering womanhood. Coming-out rituals, the Latin *quincenera*, the Jewish *bat mitzvah*, and Native American coming-of-age rituals are all such announcement parties.

The Mother. The second stage is a time of heavy responsibilities. During this stage, a woman's blood flows monthly to facilitate her bearing of children, and red is commonly accepted as the symbolic color.

The Crone. In the third and final stage, the woman embodies all life stages and experience. She is known as *Crone* and no longer loses her Sacred Blood of Wisdom but keeps it in her body to nurture and retain the strength within her. Long ago, this passage was ritualized; the Crone was welcomed as the revered elder of the circle. Until very recently such celebrations have been rare, as society has lost respect for the wisdom and understanding of aged ones in our communities.

The popularity of Croning is now becoming widespread. Women choosing to celebrate this transition also choose the time when they are ready to announce the beginning of that final stage of their lives. For me, the experience was especially rich because others joined me in the passage and we planned and carried out the ritual together. We were there for each other to celebrate the passage and to share the joy. One of the joyful items some of us added to our lives were *Certified Crone* certificates. Check the back of this book for a pull-out version of your own certificate, designed to be displayed in a three-by-five photo frame.

When Is the Right Time?

The new or waning moon phase is a traditional Crone's time, and many celebrations are conducted then. This is the last phase of the moon's cycle, just as Cronehood is the last phase of a woman's life cycle.

The later months (October, November, and December) are the most common for the ancient rite, with October being the preferred month. October is ruled by Hecate, often called the Dark Mother, who is associated with death and the end of cycles. Black is the color of darkness, symbolizing that life rests there before being born anew. The Crone stands at the gateway to death—to rebirth. To begin life again, there must first be death . . . the new moon goes on to waxing, and then to full. Death is part of the continuing cycle of wholeness. The Crone closes one cycle so that another can begin.

Ceremonial Symbols

Amethyst. The amethyst is the gem of the Crone. It is associated with spirituality and wisdom and has a history of being a symbolic element in ancient Croning rituals.

Crown. A Crone is often initiated by the placement of a crown on her head. The crown is a symbol of ascension to a higher rank—the rank of Crone. Often the crown is made by the Crone using dried flowers, branches, or whatever material is available and meaningful to the woman.

Braid. The placement of a crown may or may not be accompanied by the draping of a vestment or a braid over an initiate's shoulders. The braid may be made of four different colored ribbons. The colors represent whatever the Crone wants them to. They are commonly related to the four directions (north, south, east, and west), the four parts of a woman's life (physical, intellectual, emotional, and spiritual), or the elements (earth, air, fire, and water). Sometimes, woven into the center can be a thin black ribbon or thread, called the

Cord of Remembering, which honors all women who have gone before and reminds us of our mortality.

Ceremonial Colors

Braids, crowns, and stoles often contain the colors of the three stages of women's lives: white for the Maiden, red honoring the Mother, and black or maybe shades of purple and black for the Crone. A common color combination worn and used in decorations is purple and black.

Purple was once worn only by royalty, denoting power. As a symbol of old age, it signifies that the honored one has matured into high rank. It also represents fame, fortune, and hard work. Black is the color of the west, the unconscious, the feminine, and aging—all of which make it an appropriate choice.

Other possible color combinations are silver and purple or red and purple—there is no right or wrong choice, and there are probably as many possible combinations as there are colors. Attire at Cronings I have attended has been beautiful, celebratory, and colorful. In some cases, Crones change clothing at the end of the formal ritual to something even more personally meaningful.

Taking a New Name

An option for some Crones is to take another name.
Since many of these traditions come from the ancient
Celts, Old Europe, or native (pre-colonial) America,
some women choose a name from one of those beginnings. The choice could also be the name of an ancestor,
or perhaps an animal. The decision is purely personal.

Where Should the Ritual Take Place?

Physical space can be anything from a quiet room in
your home to a public park, a forest, desert, a place by
the seaside, a back yard, or even a public dining room.
The space you choose doesn't have to be a *permanent*
sacred place. It can be cleansed and purified with
incense, candles, sage, or whatever you have available.
Then, once the ceremony is over and life goes on, the
space reverts back to whatever it was before. It's a good
idea to designate the space as sacred when you start
your ceremony, then release it when you are finished.

Announcing Your Intentions

Croning is a very old traditional announcement to the world that the celebrant now considers herself a Crone. This makes it relevant that she also announce her intentions for this new stage of life. In determining *your* intentions, the following list may be of help. Croning signifies that it is time to:

- Love yourself completely and unconditionally
- Honor the historical significance of the Crone, wisest of women
- With pride, claim status as a Crone
- Share your collective power and wisdom
- Work to reverse ageism worldwide
- Claim and take full responsibility for passage into the next stage
- Balance male and female energies
- Examine issues within yourself
- Come to terms with the Old Hag Self
- Deal with anger, fear, depression, and the darkness within each of us

- Claim personal power
- Move from dependence to responsibility
- Accept different realities without judgment
- Speak your own mind
- Practice sovereignty—the power of your own choices—over yourself
- Find passion and make your desires happen
- Become a sister (sisterhood of women)
- Find an environment that is supportive of the old
- Make a game plan and find role models, books, and support groups to implement it
- Accept different realities and do not be judgmental
- *Find* yourself—don't just live happily ever after
- Expect chaos in this time of transition
- Expect opportunities to deal with old games and patterns
- Go into the pain and chaos to claim your own power as a Crone—take power, walk the path

What Activities Might I Incorporate?

An important element in the ritual is for the woman being Croned to have a chance to tell her story. It may be fitting for all women present to tell their stories. One formal and sharing way to do this is using the following exercise, called *Decades*.

Decades. Participating women all stand in a circle. Each in turn tells what life was like for her during her first twenty years. If she has surpassed twenty years, she moves one step toward the center of the circle as she finishes speaking. Each woman takes their turn, stepping forward if she has lived more than twenty years or remaining in place if her age doesn't surpass that decade. After all have spoken or declined to speak, the first woman describes her life between the years of twenty to thirty. If she is older than thirty, when she finishes she again steps forward. This activity continues decade by decade until the oldest women stand in the very center of the circle, surrounded and honored by the younger women. This ceremony can be adapted depending on the time available and the number of guests present.

Feasting and Dancing. Eating, singing, and dancing are popular activities accompanied by stories and anything else that the Cronee deems appropriate. At many Cronings, music is provided by the guests. Drums and rattles are usually present in abundance. Some guests may provide music with Celtic or lap harps, pipes, or other portable instruments. The most commonly used instrument is each guest's voice.

Gifts. Symbolic gifts are presented to each Crone. Three kernels of blue corn are sometimes given. The corn represents ovum, children, and creativity. Amethysts are often bestowed. Other gifts are as varied as the women who give and receive them. My daughter's gift to me was a song she wrote and sang at my Croning. I also received a raven feather tied with small beads and purple ribbon and a handmade wand. Any gift is appropriate for this gala event.

Large Group Rituals

48

Many women have had the opportunity to experience Cronings at several of the national Crone organization conferences. There is always great joy and excitement, as well as time for serious reflection and solemnity. As Malka Golden-Wolfe[4], a Crone, healer, and therapist, says:

> *There is no limit to the time a Crone may experience such a ritual. No matter how many times a woman gets Croned, each time is unique, meaningful, and an affirmation that we continue to grow and deepen. Croning is not an end in itself. It is a beginning of a new journey through wisdom's gate, a confirmation of self-acceptance and aging. A celebration and reclaiming of personal and communal worth of old women. We can not reclaim that too many times. More is better, because we need to continually remind ourselves of our new status and get rid of the old programming.*

For women interested in large group Croning, the late Shauna Adix of Crone Counsel (see page 186) provided the following information about ritual:

An integral part of every Crones Counsel is ritual. It takes many forms. There is always an evening devoted to ceremony. Daily workshops and general story-telling sessions provide discussion of or experience with rituals of various kinds. Initially the evening rit-ual took the form of a general Croning ceremony. Most recently, the gathering has provided workshop time to discuss planning and carrying out of personal Croning events. The evening ritual has become a cer-emony honoring the elders present. The local plan-ning committee determines the form of the ceremony. It involves identifying the oldest participants and oth-ers of her decade. Each succeeding decade in turn is recognized, with the younger participants honoring those older.

Reflections

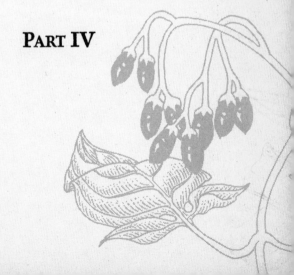

PART IV

A Croning ritual means different things to different women. As one prepares to formally announce her Cronehood, it is proper and just to look at how life will or should be different after the experience. Formally writing and speaking of one's intentions is one way of making the future more tangible. Although it may not happen in the blink of an eye, preparations need to be made for the Crone to move into her new life. Crones from all over the United States shared their delight in the changes they noticed after their ceremonies.

Wise Women, In Retrospect...

My Croning ceremony was one of the most
wonderful days of my life. This is a common
denominator. Women who have never known the
incredible support system they can get from their
sisters are truly deprived. And most often, all they
have to do is ask.

—VIRGINIA CRONE

I had no idea in advance how empowering this
ceremony would be. The honoring of my qualities
was a profound experience. I had to really stretch
to accept those affirmations of love, respect, and
honor. It was the most important ceremony I have
ever done. I encourage women to share your wisdom, embrace life, and include your death as a
meaningful approaching part of the life
you embrace.

—MIDWESTERN CRONE

I saw much of it through a blur of tears. Friendship
has always been central to my mental health and

the support friends have given me over the years has gotten me through some tough times. The heart of my Croning was friendship—women who have shared my life for many years.

—ARIZONA CRONE

Every time something happens that reflects on my age, I remember the ritual and laugh. I feel confident of my strength and have reached a point where I say what I think and don't give a damn about what people say. In many ways I'm more comfortable with this stage of my life than I was with maidenhood and motherhood. The Croning ritual truly liberated me as a woman and as a human being. The support is an anchor that will always hold.

—LAUGHING MINNESOTA CRONE

I believe in ritual. Ritual, whether religious or secular, is the glue of human society. I especially believe in rites of passage—that major rites should accompany birth, coming of age, marriage, elderhood, and death, and minor rites should mark lessor occasions. I have lamented for forty years (since I came of age as a stranger in a culture that emphasized menarche rituals for women) that our society does not provide coming-of-age initiations and ceremonies in a formal way. Small rituals of sharing on any given subject puts a rainbow of wisdom into the center for processing by all. Activity done in a cohesive group multiplies the wisdom available to any one person in the group. I believe that ritual is powerful, that group ritual is more powerful, and that a group of elders performing ritual is a force indeed. When elders accept elderhood, they take on the group job of providing the structure of the society. Elders guide the change and growth of those who follow. The Rite of Croning is an externalization, a peer recognition of one's new status as an elder, and a formal acceptance of the role of Crone. The difference between having such a rite when one reaches this age and not having one is like the difference between getting married and shacking up. A ritual. A formalization. That's all. But

somehow, putting the body through a ritual is more
'real' than when the ritual is skipped.

—CRONE WHO RECENTLY EARNED A
MASTERS OF COUNSELING

I am more accepting, more tranquil, letting go of so
many negative experiences, reordering priorities.
Since the ritual I have developed a life-threatening
illness, so I am blood-transfusion dependent.
Somehow, having crossed the threshold into
Cronedom has made that easier.

—CALIFORNIA CRONE

Magic changed my relationship with my daughter.
It brought to my attention my avoidance of talking
and thinking about age and aging. It is a natural
sequence in life and I am in this twilight time of
life. There is no logical reason why I should avoid
it. I am beginning to accept that other people are
seeing me differently. I haven't done it all yet but I
do have a lighter and softer heart. Serenity is the

answer, not placidness. I look at life through a prism. It helps me to be tolerant, to grow in love and patience. Through the magic of my Croning and my daughter's participation, we changed. It helped many negatives become positives. This experience made me aware of how important it is to reach out to younger women, to help educate them to understand our responsibilities toward the younger. I have developed a passion regarding feminine education of young women.

—CRONE WHOSE DAUGHTER
UNEXPECTEDLY ATTENDED
HER "CROWNING"

Wait with your process. You will know when it is time. Croning for me has an evolving meaning. It has been five years since my ritual and much has come to pass. It is a soul-deepening feminine rite of passage, a reclaiming of the power and wisdom of the old woman who has consciously lived her life. Trust yourselves and your beliefs about women and who we really are. Reawaken the spirit of the

Goddess within yourselves, allow Her space, time, energy, and money—whatever it takes to help Her come alive again. This being of spirit and light that is you! The world is waiting for each unique, creative, powerful woman; Maiden, Mother, and Crone. Becoming a Crone opens the door to one of our deepest archetypes without closing the door to the earlier ones. One was Maiden, then Mother, now one is Crone who remembers (embraces) being the other two. Is this not the essence of wisdom?

—A Crone's advice to Maidens

My Croning was one of the most meaningful events in my life and has underscored *me being me* as I continue on my path. Periodic depression has been part of my life. These times are still tough but that is me too. My friends occasionally refer to me as *Crone*. I like it. My self-confidence is increased. I have good things to offer and do. Croning is a conscious self-initiation into understanding that the body is spirit-made-dense and that spirit will lift from it. Realizing this [makes it clear that our]

60

responsibility as a citizen of the planet is . . . larger than daughter-wife-mother. Life is different because I realize I have let go of trying to compete in the world of work. I continue to work, but defining myself as an aging woman with new things to do allows me to let go of trying to advance in the patriarchal system. I allot more and more time to doing what I need to do to evolve into a consciously concerned citizen of the planet rather than a wage earner and materials gatherer. I am slowly identifying what it is I am supposed to be doing [in] this Crone age of my life. I am more at peace with my personal self and more aware of the states of crisis of our physical planet and societies living on it. I count myself lucky to live in a time and place where Croning is possible. I have lamented that our society does not provide coming-of-age initiations and ceremonies in a formal way. Having experienced my Croning, it became very real and very sacred because it was a physical manifestation of my internal designs.

—A THOUGHTFUL CRONE SPEAKS

I could never begin to describe what happened on a
mystical and spiritual level. I draw on the strength
of all the women in our Croning circle to help me
on the next years and add my strength to theirs as
needed. I would truly encourage women to trust the
process, and not have everything pre-planned. That
is the way of patriarchy, not a feminine way. Just
know a few things . . . have a beautiful setting, art
materials, flowers, oils, [and] drums or other
instruments. Create the sacred space, invite the
Crone and all her spirit allies in, and
watch the magic happen.

—SHARING CRONE

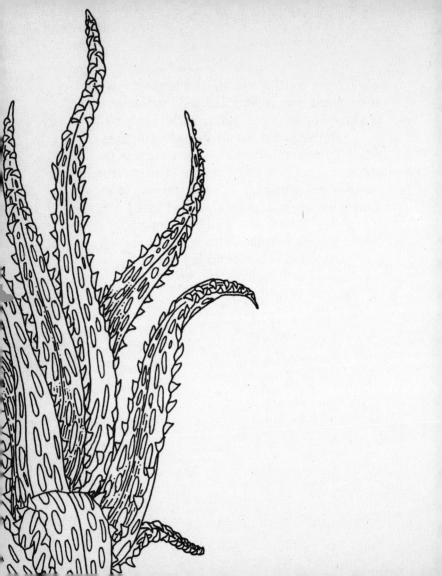

Rituals

PART V

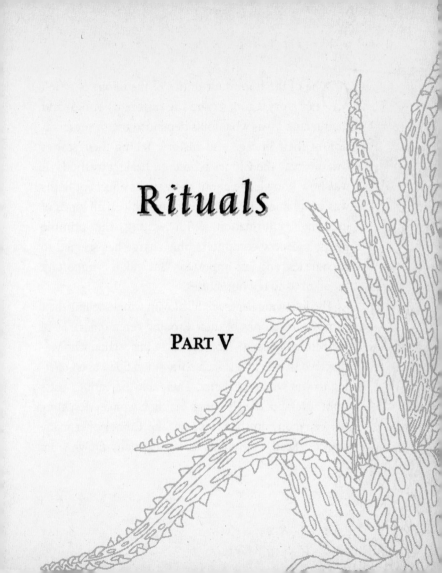

64

One of the important duties of the Crone is to tell her story. Crones were the historians of old, and their method was what folks depended on for preservation of their lineage and history. Telling their stories was one way the Crones passed on healing methods. It was how knowledge about the various effects of herbs was maintained. It was a way of passing on all kinds of important information. With writing, the printing press, and now computers, this charge has seemed to become less and less important. But still, it is important for all of us to tell our stories.

The following pages are filled with Crones telling their stories—the stories of their Croning ceremonies . . . of their formal passage. The Crones in this section who volunteered to tell of their sacred transition do so as an offering to you who come after. There may be various parts from several of the Cronings that fit a woman designing her ceremony. In their wisdom, the Crones offer many choices. Read, enjoy, and make selections drawn from

one or several of the following rituals when you design
your own ceremony.

The Basics

Many Crones choose to set up an altar in the center of a
circle to gather around for at least part of the ceremony,
if not all. Items on the altar may include:

- A feather for the element of air
- Water for the element of water
- Flowers for the element of earth
- Candle(s) for the element of fire

Variations of these symbols for the elements may be
used. For instance, sea shells for water would work, as
would a heavy container of burning charcoal or a con-
tained and supervised fire for the element of fire—use
whatever feels appropriate. The following rituals should
give you plenty of ideas.

Croning of the Wise Women...

by Ruth Gardner

The following ritual for three initiates was written with the help of two other women. It was my first exposure to a Croning ceremony. It was my own. We all belonged to Wise Women, a small spirituality group in Tucson who met bimonthly to share and drum. One member had experienced her own ceremony several years earlier in California. It was with difficulty that we searched for information to help us accomplish what follows—most of what we used were suggestions made by other women. Wise Women is no longer in existence.

For this ritual you will need:

- A small container of salt
- A bowl of grapes
- A basket of whole grain bread

{Processional}

All chant:

Where I am is holy, holy is this ground
Forest, mountain, river, listen to the sound
Great spirit circles all around me[5]

{Drumming}

Facilitator:

On this day we gather as a circle to celebrate the Croning of three of you, you who have lived long and have many earthly years of experience. To begin our celebration, let us honor Hecate, the Crone, the most ancient form of the moon goddess trinity. She is the heavenly midwife, goddess of the last quarter moon. Hecate is the woman and the cauldron, the birth in death aspect, and the center of becoming. Hecate has dominion over all endings and, therefore, all beginnings.

"Hecate":

I take away your fears of death and make you glad. I am the keeper of altars, outdoors and inside. I am speaking in you when you feel the desire to stand alone on a hillside, or in a clearing in the desert, and talk to the full moon. I am the wild part of you, your sixth sense, the one who gives you your hunches, pre-monitions, and dreams. I am the priestess immortal. My face is threefold, young, old, and in full bloom. I see ahead and behind. I am the hinge of reality. I am your primal goddess.[6]

Facilitator:

> *Honoring Hecate in oneself leads to a space of reflec-*
> *tive calm, of heightened sensitivity and awareness.*
> *Introversion and spirituality are strong now, and this*
> *is the time of learning, of developing and using psychic*
> *skills, of being in touch with our intuition. Moments of*
> *endings are new beginnings, the lesson of Hecate's*
> *darkening moon.*

Facilitator calls to the spirits of the north to be present at this ceremony. She calls to the spirits of the east to be present at this ceremony. She calls to the spirits of the south to be present at this ceremony. She calls to the spirits of the west to be present at this ceremony. She calls on the spirits of Hecate and other goddesses to be present. Then, each **Crone Initiate** speaks about what being a woman means to her at this point in her life and what her intentions are for the future. These were my words:

> *Thank you for honoring me as a Crone here today. For*
> *me, this initiation as a Crone is symbolic of death and*
> *rebirth, a rite of passage that transforms my focus in*

life from one of a physically active life to one of more thoughtful interests. It is a time of reflection, acceptance and satisfaction, a time of new responsibilities. I vow to accept these new responsibilities gracefully and do my best to understand and carry them out. I vow to use the wisdom I have wisely, to use it when asked, and not to force it on others at any time. I vow to pursue deepened personal growth, autonomy, environmental harmony, positive relationships, and greater self-acceptance. I honor and give thanks to my mother, my grandmothers, all women who have gone before me, gratitude to women of the world, and especially those present here.

71

All:

We celebrate with you the unending wisdom of your life!

{**All** sing "Woman Am I,"[7] page 170}

Each **Crone Initiate** is now crowned individually. The **Initiate's Daughter** may honor the initiate as she crowns her, such as my daughter did for me with the song she wrote and performed . . .

{**Daughter** sings "My Mother's Song,"[8] page 173}

Each **Daughter** (or surrogate daughter) takes a pinch of
salt from the altar and sprinkles it at the feet of her
mother, the **Crone Initiate**.

All:

> *Eternal Wisdom, as a woman of experience, you are
> the salt of the earth. May you know and use your wis-
> dom all the days of your life.*

Altar grapes and whole grain bread are shared, passed
by the **Facilitator**.

{Drumming}

Crones close the circle, thanking spirits and grounding
energy.

{**All** sing thrice: "Old Celtic Blessing,"[9] page 171}

This joyful event was followed by more joy and feasting
on succulent, appealing, delightful food including
elderberry pie. The ceremony was invigorating and
energizing. One Crone said it left her with a feeling of
invincibility and wisdom and yet humility. It was a life-
changing experience.

Croning for Margaret...

by Serene Fusek

Margaret Cubberly is a freelance journalist and story-teller who lives in Virginia. She writes an opinion column for a local weekly paper, studies Tai Chi and yoga, collects feathers, fans, and masks, and enjoys a circle of friends ranging from poets to herbalists. Her life revolves around her husband and daughter, two cats, and about two thousand books.

The ritual was written by Serene Fusek, poet, writer, Christian, Gnostic, Pagan. She practices ritual with a small group of friends and is the author of *Night Screams With Jaguar's Voice* (Skiff's Creek Press). She has also published *Color of Poison* (Slipstream Press). Please note that all <u>underlined</u> text is credited to Marcia Starck (see footnoted reference next to first incident of underlining).

In addition to the basics listed on page 65, you will need the following for this ritual:

- Sweet grass
- A leafy branch or wand
- A vase with three corn kernels

People are in a standing position. Songs are played on tape. **Facilitator** draws the circle with a leafy branch or a wand. **Assistant** cleanses everyone by touching them with sweet grass.

Facilitator:

> *We are gathered in this circle to help our sister, [Name], make the transition to Crone/grandmother. We are going to call the powers of the four directions, four metaphysical elements, and five goddesses to help us in this endeavor. These powers are metaphoric ways of thinking about energies and psychic states.*

Designates call the directions and the metaphysical elements in turn, one person per direction and element. After a direction is called, another designate calls a goddess associated with that direction. The woman calling a direction should stand in the corresponding part of the circle and the woman calling the goddess associated with that direction should stand next to her.

Designates in the east, in turn:

> *East, direction of the rising sun, of new beginnings, we invoke and call you to our circle.*

> *Air, element of the eagle and hawk, of the bat and the fleet, shy deer, we invoke you.*

> <u>*Kali, I call You from the eastern gate, goddess of creation and destruction, Who dances in the graveyards, You Who know of the transformation we are going through today. Be with us and help us, Kali Ma.*</u>[10]

Designates in the south, in turn:

> *South, direction of the warming breezes, land of summer, the time of growth toward harvest, we invoke you.*

> *Fire, element of passion, of transformation, we call you.*

> <u>*Oya, dark African mother, You who stand at the frontier between life and death, insatiable in Your quest for truth, we call You at the southern gate.*</u>

Designates in the west, in turn:

> *West, direction of the setting sun, of the going into night, of owl and jaguar who know the wisdom of shadows, we call you to our circle.*

76

Water, element of the sea that swallows the sun, of the rivers that carry us on journeys, of the ripples of sensitivity we invoke you.

Changing Woman, Who weaves the web of our lives and knots the times of our transits, Who transforms all She touches, we call You at the western gate. We ask that You be here with us this day.

Designates in the north, in turn:

North, direction of the north wind that brings winter, land of night and death, we call you to our circle.

Earth, that grows our food but also hides our dead, we invoke you.

Hella, Scandinavian mistress of the dead, You Who ride through the Black Forest, we invoke Your ancient wisdom.

Crone Initiate:

Hecate, Crone goddess of the dark moon, You Who understand the power and wisdom of the darkness and how it swells again to light, come into our circle and bless us.

{All sit}

Crone Reader 1:

In women's medicine traditions, one of the most powerful times in a woman's life is when she enters the Crone or Wise Woman phase, when she makes the passage to the grandmother energy.

Reader 2:

In Old English the word comes from the word "crown" and in German the word krone means "crown."

Reader 3:

The Crone is the designation of the third of the triple goddess' three aspects and represents old age, death, winter, the waning moon. The Crone represents the third, postmenopausal phase of a woman's life. Some tribes believe that women became very wise when they no longer shed the lunar "wise blood" but kept it inside. The Crone also has a fearsome destructive side as witnessed in some of the Crone goddesses: Hecate, Kali, Hella, Morgan.

Reader 1:

Because older women hold so much power, they have been revered as well as feared throughout the centuries.

Qualities of the Crone

Reader 3:

The first quality we associate with the grandmother energy or Croneship is wisdom. Older women are the keepers of the wisdom and traditions in their families, clans, tribes, covens, and communities.

Reader 2:

The primary wisdom of knowledge that the Crone has is the understanding of the two greatest mysteries, birth and death. It was the patriarchy's fears of this knowledge, the herbs, the midwifery practices, the communication with those who had departed, that led to the denigration of the Wise Woman.

Reader 3:

Another quality of the Crone is the ability to go between two worlds. This is the shapeshifting shamanistic talent that enables the Wise Woman to go "beyond the veil."

Reader 1:

When a woman leaves the mothering phase and enters grandmother consciousness, she takes on a new sense of freedom. Mothering—whether of one's physical children, clients, or friends—requires a lot of close attention and the dedication of large amounts of energy. Grandmothering, however, is different in that the grandmother's arms are wider (more wisdom) but farther away. She has paid her dues, given her time as mother, healer, therapist, counselor. And though she may continue these roles, she does so in a different way, with more detachment, with more freedom for herself.

Reader 3:

As a result of this freedom, there is a lot of creativity unleashed in this phase of life. One's responsibilities and duties on the earth have lifted and it is time to express this freedom in art, poetry, song, dance, and crafts. The creative urges that were put into mothering and caretaking have been freed up and many new doors are open.

Reader 2:

With this artistic freedom comes a sense of wildness and release. All of those things which were prohibited earlier seem possible now. One woman decided that she no longer had to dress a certain way to please her boss or to attract men so she began to dress to please herself, to express her own being and individuality.

Reader 1:

Sexual freedom is another strong experience of older women. Often bound up in marriages or by social prohibitions for much of their lives, they are now able to get in touch with their androgynous state, the balance of male and female energy, and therefore can enjoy relationships in a new way. Relationship now is based more on sharing and mutual interests, less on need and dependency.

Reader 2:

This wisdom, freedom, wildness, and self-expression can only lead to a sense of power. Power results from being true to oneself and one's own particular dharma. Power to stand up to authority figures and assert one's own worth as a woman and as an individual. Power to pursue any avenue in life, even where doors seemed closed before. Power to make boundaries and to say no when one should.

Reader 3:

Power to be and exist, which is to tap into the universal energy, and to know that one is truly part of a larger cosmic support system. This, perhaps, is the core meaning of grandmother consciousness and Crone wisdom.

Responsibilities of the Crone

Reader 1:

The first responsibility of this phase of womanhood is to nurture oneself. Only by nurturing oneself can one nurture others and Mother Earth. Nurturing means attending to all one's needs, physical, emotional, spiritual. It means eating good, nutritious food. It means exercising one's body, having massage and other relaxing treatments. It means seeking relationships that are supportive. It means being involved in activities that are mentally satisfying and stimulating.

Reader 2:

When a woman is nurtured herself, then she can attend to others and the needs of the Great Mother—

the Earth. Then she can use her wisdom to support change and growth in her sisters and brothers, to attune others to the plight of the planet. As a source of wisdom, the Crone can help younger women to understand their role, to balance their bodies; she can instruct them on the purposes and functions of relationships, motherhood, and their duties to their community or tribe.

83

Reader 3:

Perhaps most importantly, she bears the responsibility to be beautiful—physically, emotionally, spiritually. It is the Crone, the grandmother, who represents the Great Earth Mother, the Goddess. She needs to portray the Goddess with every step she takes, with every thought she thinks, with every action she makes. The Navajo say "Walk in beauty" and this is truly the key to grandmother energy, Crone consciousness.

Facilitator walks to the circle's center and calls the **Initiate**. She gives **Initiate** three corn kernels and says:

The first seed is for the ova that have passed through you. The second seed is for children you have birthed.[11] The third seed is for all your creative projects.

84

The **Initiate** returns to the circle with the seeds. **Each Woman** shares something learned about aging that is positive—older women from experience, younger women from a poem or something said to them by an older woman. The **Initiate** comes back to circle center and places the kernels in a waiting vase with a prayer or wish for each one. The other women of the circle stand, form a bridge of hands around the circle that breaks at the north, and pass her through. When she reaches the break in the hands, she is standing at the north of the circle—the direction of death and transformation.

Facilitator (giving Initiate the items as she speaks):

A sip of wine for the blood . . . . A sip of honey for the sweetness of this phase of your life.

A **Chosen Woman** crowns the **Initiate**. The **Initiate** announces her new name, should she have chosen one, and the circle of many repeats it back to her.

All chant:

> *We are sisters on a journey*
> *Singing in the sun*
> *Singing in the darkest night*
> *The healing has begun, begun*
> *The healing has begun*
>
> *We are sisters on a journey*
> *Singing now as one*
> *Remembering the ancient ones*
> *The women and their wisdom*
> *The women and their wisdom*

The **Facilitator** releases all of the directions, elements, and goddesses. The circle is broken, and the newly crowned Crone plants her three seeds on or during the next full moon.

Croning for Desert Crones...

by Ruth Gardner

Desert Crones is an organization in Arizona which affirms understanding of the aging process of women over fifty as they share, enlighten, and celebrate the vibrant fulfillment of old womanhood. The following was written with input from Caitlin Williams. It is meant to be used for multiple Crone initiates and performed by a group on their behalf.

A guitarist plays women's music and sings and hums softly. **Facilitator** casts the circle, calling the elements and directions.

Calling Earth (North)

Facilitator speaks the following words, then **Everyone** repeats them in unison. **Facilitator** dances toward the north, beckoning the spirits of the north to follow her back into the circle. **All** follow her movements.

> *We approach the north and ask that the guardians and blessings symbolized by this direction be with us tonight. Greetings and blessed be the most ancient Crone mothers of the north. One spirit in many manifestations, we invite you to be with us tonight.*

Facilitator:

Special Crone mother, Tlazalteotl [Tlawz-al-tay-o-tl], mother confessor, eater of filth, cleanser, purifier!

Changing Woman—living Crone mother of our land, teacher of cycles: birth, youth, aging, and death, mother of guardians!

Teocinte—grandmother of our blessed corn!

Gaia—primeval goddess and Mother Earth, and all the clan mothers of the totems of the north, guard the stanchions of the north and be with us tonight!

Calling Air (East)

Facilitator speaks the following and **Everyone** repeats in unison. **Facilitator** dances toward the east, beckoning those spirits to follow her back into the circle. **All** follow.

We approach the east and ask that the guardians and blessings symbolized by this direction be with us tonight. Greetings and blessed be the most ancient Crone mothers of the east. One spirit in many manifestations, we invite you to be with us tonight.

Facilitator:

90

> Spider Woman—ancient Crone mother, bringer of culture and technology Who has become the very spirit of and weaver of realities!

> Baba Yaga—grandmother Crone, wise witch of women's secrets!

> Tzin Tzin Tzin—ancient grandmother hummingbird, symbol of our uniqueness, the air in the wing!

> Aiyazan—most ancient Crone of all initiations, bearer of the rainbow, symbol of our unity in diversity, and all the clan mothers of the totems of the east, guard the stanchions of the east and be with us tonight.

Calling Fire (South)

Facilitator speaks the following and **Everyone** repeats in unison. **Facilitator** dances toward the south, beckoning those spirits to follow her back into the circle. **All** follow.

> We approach the south and ask that the guardians and blessings symbolized by this direction be with us tonight. Greetings and blessed be the most ancient

Crone mothers of the south. One spirit in many man-
ifestations, we invite you to be with us tonight.

Facilitator:

White Buffalo Woman—the fire in the bowl. Bringer
of the pipe of peace, given to all nations by the recent
birth of Your daughter!

Pele—the fire in the earth. Mother of passion and
power, creatress of new life!

Oya—Crone of the tree of all ancestors, mother of
transformation, owner of the broom of the clean
sweep. Ruler of boundaries of change and exchange!

Hecate—most ancient Crone mother of life, death, and
reincarnation, guardian of the threefold path, and all
the clan mothers of the totems of the south, guard the
stanchions of the south and be with us tonight.

Calling Water (West)

Facilitator speaks the following and **Everyone** repeats in
unison. **Facilitator** dances toward the west, beckoning
those spirits to follow her back into the circle. **All** follow.

We approach the west and ask that the guardians and blessings symbolized by this direction be with us tonight. Greetings and blessed be the most ancient Crone mothers of the west. One spirit in many manifestations, we invite you to be with us tonight.

Facilitator:

Chihaucoatl [Shi-wa-coat-el]—most ancient mother Crone of living waters, wearer of the skirt of serpents!

Sedna—old Crone woman of the sea, heart of woman's power!

Olokun—ancient Crone of deep water, guardian of the greatest treasure, the collective unconscious!

Kuan Yin—most ancient Crone mother, bearer of the tides of life, and all the clan mothers of the totems of the west guard the stanchions of the west and be with us tonight.

Calling Spirit (Center)

Facilitator speaks the following and **Everyone** repeats in unison. **Facilitator** dances toward the center, beckoning those spirits to follow her back into the circle. **All** follow.

We approach the center and ask that the guardians and blessings symbolized by this direction be with us tonight. Greetings and blessed be the most ancient Crone mothers of the center. One spirit in many manifestations, we invite you to be with us tonight.

Facilitator:

Tonantzin—most ancient Crone mother of the gods, mother of saviors, patroness, protectress of this blessed land of Anahuac where we reside!

Blessed cauldron Crone mother, Cerridwin—guardian of the double helix spiral, mysteries of life, death and rebirth!

Shekhinah—most ancient mother of the Holy Spirit!

Inanna—most ancient mother of Creation Herself! Be with us, bless us here, now, and forever.

Crone 1:

We see the shape of each woman's story—its sorrows, pain, joy, aspirations, and achievements.

Participants form a circle. **Crone 1** leads the group in a *Decades* exercise (see page 46), encouraging participants to be concise and, in the event that they choose not to speak of a decade, to say only "I survived."

Crone 2 (to Initiates):

Welcome to the Sisterhood of Crones! Joining the Sisterhood of Crones is a milestone. Now is the time to be joyous, to be proud you have attained many years of living on Mother Earth. Wisdom is your crown. Discover and share its thousands of jewels. Gather the robe of experience around your shoulders. Wear the purple dress of honor for your unique self and precious lace woven of power, humility, and love to protect our limbs. Humor shines out of hooded eyes; the voice of the raven is gentle but persistent. Celebrate the autumn years as if it is springtime. Be creative, courageous, and colorful. Welcome to the Sisterhood!

Crone 1 distributes scrolls containing parchments of the group's welcome and intentions. These documents are unique to each Croning group.

Crone 3:

In this formal Croning celebration, I read a group intention for all being Croned:

I announce my intentions for my future as a Crone: to celebrate the awareness of my aging process and to know from this place in time I can review my past and look forward to my continuing growth mentally, physically, and spiritually; to give of my wisdom, strength, and talent where it is needed; to join the elders and other Crones in affirming our place in creating new attitudes of respect toward growth and aging. I give thanks to my female ancestors as well as gratitude to all women of the world, and especially to the women gathered here today.

Crone 4:

Women of experience, you are the salt of the earth. Know and use your wisdom wisely.

Crone 4 repeats these words as she sprinkles salt at the feet of each **Crone Initiate**.

{**Crone 5** sings "Ancient Mother,"[12] page 174}

As she sings, **Crone 5** drapes a braid around the shoulders of each **Crone Initiate**. The braids have been woven to honor all the strands of experience that the

Crones have woven into their rich lives. Next, **Two Crones** join arms to form an arch before the **Initiates**.

Crone 6:

> *Be aware that as you dance through this arch, you dance into new and strengthened lives. Your wisdom will stand you in good stead as you listen, share, and love in greater abundance than before.*

The **Crone Initiates** dance through the arch, a symbolic birthing channel, to their new lives as Crones.

{**All** sing "River of Birds,"[13] page 172}

The ceremony ends with a celebration—everyone enjoys drumming, dancing, and feasting.

Solitary Croning...

by Ruth Gardner

I wrote this ceremony to encourage readers who may hesitate to ask others to join in this solemn ritual. The passage from the phase of Motherhood to Cronehood is so important that all women need a chance to participate whether they conduct their own private, personal ritual or decide to join with others.

In addition to the basics listed on page 65, you need the following for this ritual:

- Four candles (white, red, purple or black, and a fourth color of your choice)
- A dish of salt
- A bowl of water
- Favorite crystals or stones
- An empty metal tray or dish
- Paper upon which you have written a list of intentions for yourself as a new Crone

Crone Initiate:

> *I call on the east, on Spider Woman, to join this circle, to protect and guard me throughout this ritual.*

> *I call on the south, on Pele, to join this circle, to protect and guard me throughout this ritual.*

> *I call on the west, on Changing Woman, to join this circle, to protect and guard me throughout this ritual.*

> *I call on the north, on Gaia, to join this circle, to protect and guard me throughout this ritual.*

> *I call on the center, (spirit), on Kuan Yin, Inanna, and Shekhinah to join this circle, to protect and guard me throughout this ritual.*

Prepare to light the candles on your altar. As you light each candle, dedicate it.

Crone Initiate:

> *I light this white candle for the Maidens who have been, are, and will be.*

> *I light this red candle for the Mothers who have been, are, and will be.*

I light this purple [or black] candle for the Crones who have been, are, and will be.

I light the final candle for the spirit of all women everywhere for all time.

Crone mother, be present now. I call upon you for guidance as I strive for growth and wisdom. Help me with [list intentions]. If these are not for the greatest good, then I humbly request and await your direction. I offer to the universe my dreams and intentions. By air, I create the seed. By fire, I warm it. By water, I nourish it. By earth, I cause it to grow. From spirit, I draw the power that makes all things possible.

Place a crown of dried flowers on your own head.

Crone Initiate:

I crown myself Crone. In so doing, I affirm my status as a Crone for now and until I leave this earth. I respectfully call on the Wise Women within and without to come forth and be present in my life now and always.

You may now call on goddesses, ancestors, or women you particularly admire for their portrayal of characteristics *you* want to have as a Crone by stating their names. Next, light the paper containing your list of intentions over the center candle. Hold it over the metal tray or dish and allow it to burn as you say the following words.

Crone Initiate:

The enclosed intentions easily become part of my life.

As a new Crone, you may now choose to meditate on your new self, your intentions, the ways of your future, or whatever else seems appropriate to you. When you are finished, it is time to close the circle with the following words.

Crone Initiate:

Thanks be to all present here today, to the four directions, the elements, to the Wise Women, to my Wise Women ancestors and the spirits. So be it.

Croning Friends...

by Sara Dagg

The following ritual is a Croning for Pat Watkins and Mary Burns. It was written for two initiates by Sara Dagg, who lives in Minnesota and is interested in women's rituals and women's spirituality, and was contributed by Watkins. Please note that <u>underlined</u> sections in this ritual are excerpted from a book by Meridel Le Sueur (see the footnoted reference next to first incident of underlined text).

Pat Watkins lives in a log cabin in rural Minnesota. She has spent sixty-seven years working as a teacher and counselor, has been a salesperson, mother, and wife. She bicycles, swims, writes poetry, and has always been a seeker—which will continue, she says, "until I'm dust." She uses her Crone power regularly.

Mary Burns taught school for thirty years, then became a registered nurse. Her adventures include becoming a vegetarian, running and finishing a marathon, and serving as president of her co-op apartment association. She enjoys the outdoors, her community, camping, music, dance, family, and long-time friends.

In addition to an altar and the basics listed on page 65, for this ritual you will need the following:

- Altar candles for each direction, lit beforehand
- Yellow menopause candle, lit beforehand
- Two large red candles
- Two black candles
- Two white candles
- Two purple candles
- Several other candles arranged in a large circle around the group
- Two bowls of earth
- Garlands of flowers
- Shawls
- Prepared food on trays
- Six tokens for each initiate (these should be coins or articles belonging to the initiate)
- Two hand-held bells
- Two decorated chairs to serve as thrones
- Two purple mantles
- Two crowns

The ritual begins with the casting of the circle. Then:

Facilitator:

This ritual occurs when a woman has reached the point in her life when her Saturn has returned twice to her natal point. This happens to everyone between the ages of fifty-six and fifty-eight. Saturn is the teaching planet, slow and complete. We celebrate the effects of this celestial event on the woman's life by the Croning ritual.[14]

Reader 1:

Women have intuitively known what is needed in interpersonal behavior patterns and moral codes, encouraging the optimum quality of life for their children and their society. But this kind of knowing needs formal expression before it can become universally meaningful.

Reader 2:

At fifty-six [-seven, -eight], one is a young Crone, still experiencing the death of self as Mother. This is sometimes a time for introspection or a time apart. The Crone advances into a relationship with her new self, or actually her old self freed from the responsibili-

*ties of creation or motherhood. This new Wise Woman
is the guardian of death and spiritual life.*

Reader 3:

*The Crone initiation requires facing two deaths: the
self as Mother has died, and personal physical death
is closer. Facing these deaths is difficult, but the
process liberates the Crone to fuller life as she enters
the circle where life and death are one.*

Reader 4:

Meridel Le Sueur's Winter Prairie Woman *speaks of
the two deaths as "windows":*

<u>*Rocking, she could see the two windows. Rocking back-
ward the window and the winter bones of the old lilac
appeared. Rocking forward she waited for the wolves
to pass the front window by the door and she could see
the black skeleton of the orchard trees thrust into the
white snow.*</u>[15]

The **Youngest Participant** lights two red candles from
the large circle of candles and says the following words.

Youngest Participant:

These red candles represent creation and motherhood.

The **Oldest Participant** lights the black and white candles from the yellow menopause candle.

Oldest Participant:

> *This black candle represents earth, physical death, and fertile possibility or dark seed. This white candle represents death as spiritual life or oneness.*

Facilitator (to Crone Initiates):

> *Hold your right hand out in front of you. Look at it carefully as you say: 'This is the hand of life. This is the hand of beginnings.' Imagine that you hold yourself, as Mother, in the palm of your right hand.*

Crone Initiates (right hand raised):

> *This is the hand of life. This is the hand of beginnings.*

Facilitator:

> *Hold your left hand out in front of you. Look at it carefully as you say: 'This is the hand of death. This is the hand of endings.' Imagine that you hold yourself, as Crone, in your left hand.*

Crone Initiates (left hand raised):

> *This is the hand of death. This is the hand of endings.*

{Pause}

Crone Initiates (both hands raised):

I am readying myself to become one who walks with death. Though death is a gift that is feared, it is the gift that enables the continuum of life. The seed must fall to the ground to grow. As woman it is my privilege to give life and call myself Mother. As woman, it is my duty to embrace death and call myself Crone.[16]

Very slowly, the **Crone Initiates** bring their hands together, palms up, and then fold them—the left hand moves on top, turning the right hand down.

Crone Initiates:

I give death to myself as Mother.

Each **Crone Initiate** snuffs out her red candle with the fingers of her left hand, then places her right hand in the bowl of earth beside her.

Crone Initiates:

I claim my power as Crone.

Facilitator and Crones (to Initiates):

Are you ready to walk with death?

Crone Initiates:

We will walk with death in this life.

Reader 5:

<u>*She rose thinking of making it to the newel post, lifting*</u>
<u>*herself up to the warm beds of embracing, but she fell*</u>
<u>*back and the chair rocked her dead body until it*</u>
<u>*stopped and she sat, her long bones of the arms reach-*</u>
<u>*ing out. She saw the wolves stop.*</u>

Reader 6 (to Crone Initiates):

*You are now the Crone Initiates. You carry with you
the fearful potential for death, including social and
psychological death through rejection or abandon-
ment. Ancient religions have a place for this dark
woman who walks with death in the cycle of life:
every day has its night. But in our death-denying culture, you are denied.*

Crone Initiates put dirt on each other's faces as a chant
begins. The chant gets louder. **Initiates** are pushed out
of the circle and taken to a prepared dark sanctuary.
Each **Initiate** carries candles, one black and one white.

When they reach the sanctuary, a door or barrier keeps them out. A **Spirit Guide** (chosen Crone) helps them find tokens of experience (articles belonging to the **Crone Initiates** which have been hidden at the site) to prove them worthy of entering the sanctuary. Meanwhile, other Crones employ spoken words:

Various Readers, in turn:

Old witch, old witch, living in a dirty ditch.

Bag lady, bag lady!

You're too old, you can't do it!

She couldn't keep her husband.

Let someone younger do it.

Get out of my way.

Mom, just wear a little make-up—please?

It's too late for you—spinster!

He died of his widow's curse.

After fifty, you lose it.

Even Jesus rejected his mother.

{Pause}

Facilitator:

> *Prepare for the welcoming celebration!*

All decorate the room behind the "barrier" with flowers, beautiful food, garlands, shawls, etc.

> {**All** sing "The Earth, the Air, the Fire, the Water,"[17] page 172}

Crone Initiates knock on the door or barrier.

Facilitator:

> *Who are you wanderers?*

Crone Initiates:

> *We are women of wholeness. We are the Crones.*

Facilitator:

> *How have you come here?*

Crone Initiates:

> *We have felt our way along paths of energy from those who have gone before and those coming after us. We are like water following the ancient river's channel.*

Facilitator:

What do you want?

Crone Initiates:

Our rightful place of respect in the circle of life.

All:

Come in! Come in!

The group forms an arch of flowers through which **Crone Initiates** enter. The **Youngest Participant** leads **Initiates** through the arch as the group sings.

{**All** sing a song or chant of **Initiates'** choice}

The dirt is washed off of the **Initiates'** faces with rose water after they enter the circle.

Facilitator:

Have you brought tokens from your journey to offer to the spirits that will bless you?

Crone Initiates:

We have brought tokens.

Facilitator:

Call forth the spirit blessing.

{Drumming}

After each of the following six blessings, the **First Crone Initiate** places a token on the altar. When she has placed all of her tokens on the altar, the blessings are repeated and the **Second Crone Initiate** follows suit.

{**All** sing a song or chant of **Initiates'** choice}

All:

Spirit of the east, bring death and new life among us. Spirits of the south, bring change and passion to life. Spirits of the west, guard our going forth and our returning. Spirits of the north, inform our silence. Spirits above, guide our path. Spirits below, keep us strong in our hearts, reveal truth.

Designated Reader (from Proverbs 9: 1-6):

Wisdom hath builded her house,
she hath hewn out her seven pillars:
she hath killed her beasts;
she hath mingled her wine;

she hath also furnished her table.
She hath sent forth her maidens:
she crieth upon the highest places of the city,
Whoso is simple, let him turn hither:
as for him that wanteth understanding, she saith to him,
Come, eat of my bread,
and drink of the wine which I have mingled.
Forsake the foolish, and live;
and go in the way of understanding.

With their white and black candles together, the **Crone Initiates** light their purple candles and each then rings a bell. When both are done, they extinguish their white and black tapers.

Crone Initiates:

I light this candle of spiritual life and will keep it with me as a reminder of the blessings of life and death, in the great circle of all creation.

Facilitator:

With these blessings are you ready to accept the mantle of Crone in this community?

Crones give each **Crone Initiate** a purple mantle.

Crone Initiates:

> What is the meaning of this mantle?

All:

> That is for you to declare!

Crone Initiates sit on prepared "thrones." Designated **Crown Bearers** approach, crowning the **Initiates**.

Crown Bearers (in turn):

> Accept the crown of Croning and speak its meaning for you.

Each **Crone Initiate** speaks in turn, telling the stories of her tokens as well as speaking of Cronehood's meaning for her. Then:

Reader 1:

> _She thought she heard the wild geese passing through her. This great flight and the rising and continuation and the certainty of it warmed her. The flow, the flight and the light, the wonder of the flow and pleasure now, all generosity and love and bliss and the grace of its certainty returning, feed the fire. Live on the edge of bud from the cold corpse._

Reader 2:

And tears came to his eyes and a strange unusual sweep of understanding at the generosity of women endlessly rocking. 'By God,' he cried, 'kept us all alive. All the disasters, world wars, depressions.' He felt he should get in his cart and run back with the news from house to house. 'She escaped,' he cried. 'She escaped them.' She's joined the women going over the prairie. The great curved earth and the round moon count the days and nights, every one a growth, a movement, becoming, curving like the mounded earth, the closing of the circle, the covering of the furrow, a great round.

All (to Initiates):

Bless you with good health, happiness, long life and peaceful death. We honor you as Crones. Walk in wisdom. Be yourselves freely and outrageously. Ho. Ah-Shah.

{Dance}

All (with dance):

O Holy Ah-shah! Thou art the tree of life. Living in the middle of the eternal seed.

Facilitator:

In the ancient past, in the days of the matriarchy, and in some matrifocal cultures yet, the woman who had completed her menopausal metamorphosis initiated young men into the ways of love play most pleasing to women. She was honored as the teller of truth and the keeper of peace. She was the keeper of traditions and the link to the spirit world.[18]

Folklore has it that Crones bring good luck when you see them on the streets, for if they smile on you, you will have a very good day. They appear in important times to show the grace of the Goddess. Crones' wishes must be respected, for the Goddess demands this from the younger generation. Crones enjoy special favors, their magic is stronger, their spells are faster, their loves are stronger.

Facilitator:

Now is the time of special gifts. Now is your time for special favors.

Crone Initiates may be seated on thrones. Music is performed and gifts given. Food, fun, and merriment follow.

Croning for Joni...

by Joni Troutner

Joni Troutner, an ambitious Crone, spent her early years as an elementary teacher having achieved a masters in education. At age forty she started teaching at Pima College and at sixty became an accomplished motivational speaker—and ventriloquist! She lives in Arizona and, between her speaking engagements, works part-time as a beautician and hair stylist.

The following ritual is written as a narrative, describing her very personal Croning ritual. It can be used as a model to write your own ceremony.

The ritual began as guests gathered under the trees by my home for *Decades* (see page 46). Afterward, participants formed a processional that wound down a large number of steps decorated with candles and incense to a desert wash below, then walked across the wash and up a hill to a small cove surrounded with Palo Verde trees. Herein stood the altar.

On the altar were five generations of signed pictures of my female ancestors, small pieces of jewelry handed down to me by some of those women, flowers, stones, and candles.

The observers lined the path and I ascended through them led by my daughter, who carried a small pillow on which my handmade crown rested. I read a testament of my journey and visions of the future: a poem that I wrote entitled "Ode to the Crone" (the poem appears in the *Resources* section of this book, on page 165).

My daughter then read the following acknowledgment of thanksgiving, then placed the crown on my head.

Mom, you gave me the great miracle of life. I thank you for this. You generously shared your life with me . . . education, experiential learning, people—all types of interesting people—especially the women friends, art, excellence and detail, language and travel. My hopes for you: peace within, self-acknowledgment, trust in the 'empty' space (which is really full). Continue the magic of life and seeking universality. Always my deepest love for you.

Many friends made loving statements of their memories of my life. Drums, flutes, and rattles played as the recessional led back through the Palo Verde, across the wash, up the candle- and incense-lined steps to an open patio for a sit-down feast by a fishpond. As dusk deepened, the stars began to twinkle and that glorious feminine symbol shone in all her moon glory on the joyful group.

Nell's Croning...

by Nell Robie

The following narrative about her own Croning ritual was written for and by Nell Robie with contributions from Antiga. Nell Robie lives in a co-housing development in Minnesota. Prior to retirement and Cronehood, Nell was a teacher in a parent-choice alternative elementary school. Nell has four grown sons living in other states at present, and loves gardening and watercolor painting.

My intent to create a Croning ceremony grew over the past several years, and now it has happened.

When my guests had gathered, I told them that I considered this as important as any event in my life—my wedding, my funeral, my graduations—even *more* important than any of them. Though I'd read accounts of Cronings and avidly followed a friend's reports of her celebration, this was a first for me and I wanted it to be my very own. So I let the design of this ritual evolve gradually as it came to me, one piece at a time.

Clearly the Autumnal Equinox was the point in this (my sixty-eighth) year to claim *Crone*. I mailed the invi-

The procession returned to the house, where the fireplace was blazing warmly. My guests and witnesses stood in a circle around me as I received my crown of dried flowers, silver ribbon, and rhinestone tiara, dressed now in flowing hand-painted blue silk. Antiga sang "bless you, my sister" to me—now an official Crone.

"I honor you for your power," she said. The circle repeated the blessing, adding a recitation of attributes until the glow of my happiness burst into dance. Antiga closed the circle and I led the group singing "my" song:

Today, while the blossoms still cling to the vine . . .

Friends stepped forward to dance me around inside the circle of love we had all created.

In the dining room a feast awaited. I had festooned the mantle and lavender-covered tables with vines, wild asters, sunflowers, and harvest vegetables, and had made a huge pot of minestrone and baked squash. There was good bread and fruit. The table overflowed with potluck offerings, the fireplace blazed light and warmth (as did we). Looking around at dear friends enjoying each other, my happiness knew no bounds.

A Different Croning...

by Connie Spittler

Connie Spittler wrote and produced the "Wise Women" series, a videotape collection in national distribution that focuses on wisdom and contributions of age. She is a writer, film producer, teacher/lecturer, founding member of Desert Crones, wife, mother, and grandmother.

The most freeing idea of creating a Croning ceremony is that there is no right or wrong way to enjoy this rite of passage. Though most celebrations are women-only events, I wanted my husband of thirty-eight years to be part of honoring my years. Like tribes of old, I wanted a generational ceremony with my three daughters and my son and sons-in-law there to learn and understand the significance of the Crone. My heart needed my grandchildren—two girls and one boy—to participate in completing this circle of age.

To my surprise, the event turned multicultural when my Hispanic neighbor presented me with a *cascarone*— a beautifully decorated hollowed-out egg filled with confetti and fitted into a colorful paper wand. In her culture, the children honor their elders by tapping them on the head with the magical egg, letting the joyful confetti fly. Then a Native American friend suggested opening the ceremony by calling the four directions—an inspiring grounding ritual that always connects me with the earth and the past. My grandchildren joined me in this ceremony.

I led my loved ones in a discussion about our family history, their remembrances, their thoughts, and their contributions, focusing on the contributions of women family members in their lives. My family gave me a beautiful glass egg. Folded inside were their words of love and gratitude. I felt the urge to walk into the sea calling the names of powerful women of the past.

We toasted the Crone and the future with a special beer, home-brewed by my son.

I did it all. I did what I wanted. And that truly honors the spirit of the Crone. Strong. Individual. Memorable Old Woman. My ritual was my doorway to aging. It always brings joyful tears to my eyes to re-live this remarkable celebration.

Croning for Joan...

by Joan Weiss Hollenbeck

Joan Weiss Hollenbeck was an instructor of literature at Irvine Valley Community College as well as writing at Coastline Community College. The author of six books, she lived in California with her musician-husband. She had five children and one grandchild. Crone Joan left the earth after severe illness shortly before this book went to press.

A very good friend and I planned our ceremony together. We were both turning sixty-seven—now was the time to celebrate ourselves and join the elders.

We began with a hot tub, segued into a silent meditation (how difficult for women to stop talking), then relaxed into a potluck dinner. Later, outside under a November full moon, we sat in a drumming circle and each offered tribute to our mentors. As each woman finished speaking, we beat our drums for closure. I used an elk-hide drum made for me by a shaman. My bag of crystals lay at my feet.

Again indoors, in front of a roaring fire, my friend and I Croned each other following the eldering ritual in Marianne Williamson's *Illuminata*. I wore a pink-fringed scarf over purple and my heart opened as my friend described me—mother of three, grandmother of one, author of six books, survivor of a devastating divorce, veteran of two decades of college teaching, remarriage, and foreign travel. Thirty women joined hands to conclude the ceremony. I read from Carl Jung:

> *We cannot live in the afternoon of life according to the program of life's morning. For what was great in the morning of our lives will be little at evening. What was true in the morning will by evening become a lie.*

We then enjoyed a deep meditation and a poem of mine, "Pillows" (refer to the *Resources* section, page 166).

The ritual ended with laughing, singing, and celebrating. What a wondrous experience—a true rite of passage to enter the elder years, a time of speaking our wisdom and celebrating our age.

A Ritual to Honor...

by Shekhinah Mountainwater

Shekhinah Mountainwater is a foremother of today's burgeoning womanspirit movement and author of the classic *Ariadne's Thread: A Workbook of Goddess Magic* (Crossing Press, 1991). She is widely known for her music, her rituals, myths, calendars, tarot deck and woman runes.[20]

In addition to an altar, you will need the following:

- A gray altar cover
- A Dark Goddess image (Hecate, Kali, Cerridwen, Selket, or Persephone)
- Images of human grandmothers
- Autumn decorations (turning leaves, pumpkins, nuts, pomegranate seeds, etc.)
- Three candles, colors of choice
- Large "Mother Candle" lit beforehand
- A crown
- A special chair ("throne")

This is a ritual to honor the first silver hairs, the first wrinkles, and (or) the cessation of moonblood flow.

The altar is draped in gray and displays an image of one of the Dark Goddesses plus various human grandmothers. Signs of autumn are used to decorate. There are three candles laid in readiness for lighting by the woman who is Croning. One is for the years she has lived, one is for now, and one is for the years to come. A large Mother Candle is lit ahead of time. A special chair is arranged beside the altar (perhaps a throne?) for the Croning Woman, who now waits beyond the circle.

The women stand in a circle before the altar, holding hands and chanting the Goddess names (above), then chanting the name of the woman who is Croning. Two make a gateway for her by raising clasped hands in an archway, and invite her to enter the sacred sphere. As she passes through, they kiss her and bid her welcome.

A Priestess speaks:

Sister, now you have entered the Gateway
Of the Winter of your life.
We ask that the Crone Goddesses
Open their arms to you
And welcome you with love and peace.

All respond:

As we weave it, so shall it be.
As we weave it, so shall it be.
As we weave it, so shall it be.

The Croning Woman says:

I thank you, beloved sisters, for welcoming me to this circle, and helping me to cross this wondrous threshold of my Croning.

The First Candle and Journal

The **Croning Woman** steps to the altar to light the first candle, saying:

I honor myself, and give thanks to you, Goddess [adds anyone else she wishes to acknowledge] *for the years that I have lived.*

The **Croning Woman** lights the candle in the flame of the Mother Candle, then seats herself beside the altar. **All** are seated. A woman of advanced years (an **Elder**) comes forward with a gift to commemorate the **Croning Woman's** past: a journal in which the women have previously written their memories of her.

The Elder:

> *Sister, we wish to gift you with this memento of the*
> *road on which you have walked until now. I call upon*
> *Mnemosyne [Nem-ah-si-nee], Goddess of All*
> *Memory. Please bless [Croning Woman's name],*
> *this circle, and this book.*

The **Elder** holds the book aloft for a moment, then to
her heart. **All** the women chant Mnemosyne's name.
Then the **Elder** reads a passage aloud from the journal.
She passes it around the circle for others to read passages
they have written, phrases that give honor and remem-
brance to the **Croning Woman**, things she has said and
done that were especially wonderful, helpful, poignant,
funny, delightful, courageous, loving, and so on. There is
also room here for improvisation by women who may
not have written in the journal but wish to say something. The **Woman Who Reads Last** then rises to present the journal to the **Croning Woman**, saying:

> *As the Goddesses of Fate do weave our lives with*
> *words, so may you continue to weave words of wis-*
> *dom, beauty, love, and joy within these pages; may*
> *they be filled with wonderful memories.*

The **Croning Woman** receives the journal. She reads a passage, tells a story, or recounts something from her past that she finds significant and wishes to share. When she is finished, she holds the book aloft and to her heart, thanks Mnemosyne and any other goddesses or beings she may wish, then places the book upon the altar.

All respond:

> *As we seed it, sow it is.*
> *As we seed it, sow it is.*
> *As we seed it, sow it is.*

The Second Candle

The **Croning Woman** now prepares to light the second candle for the present, saying:

> *I thank my Goddess and my own deep self, my beloved sisters, and all those I love for this present moment in time, which is born of what has gone before and is the seed of what is to come. Let this time be blessed.*

She lights the second candle in the flame of the first, then takes her seat.

The Crown

A **Woman of Middle Years** comes forward with a garland to crown the **Croning Woman**. This can be made ahead of time out of appropriate leaves, flowers, and other decorations that represent the occasion, as well as the **Croning Woman's** unique character and taste. The **Woman of Middle Years** places the crown on the **Croning Woman's** head, saying:

Sister, we honor you as elder. May the Goddess and all those you love and your own deep self within bless you on this holy day.

All respond:

Let [Croning Woman] be blessed!
Let [Croning Woman] be blessed!
Let [Croning Woman] be blessed!

All:

Blessed be the Maiden within me, for she bringeth courage and freedom. Blessed be the Mother within me, for she bringeth love and life. Blessed be the Crone within me, for she bringeth wisdom and understanding.

The Third Candle

144

The **Croning Woman** now lights the third candle in the flame of the second, saying:

With this flame I light up my future with promise and beauty and fulfillment. May I continue to walk the pathways I have chosen in health and love, in courage and freedom, in satisfaction and self-discipline, in fun and foolishness, in peace and passion. Hecate, Kali-Ma, Cerridwen, [add other names that feel appropriate] please bless my remaining years.

All respond:

It is so.
It is so.
It is so.

The **Priestess** comes forward, saying:

Sister, in the elder time of your life you may have both more and less responsibilities.

May the Goddess gift this time for you with playfulness and fun, creativity and re-creation, rest and dreaming, magic and mystery.

And may She also bless you with the recognition you deserve for who you are and all that you have experienced and shared, assuring that you will always have a place in your community as wise one, teacher, giver of counsel, or any other of your fine skills that you choose to share.

And so we have prepared for you our offerings to help along the way.

The Giftings

A **Young Maiden** rises to present her gift, then each member of the circle follows. Gifts can be practical or frivolous, including tools and materials the **Croning Woman** can use in her life as well as playful delights. She could also receive a massage or footbath, get taken out to dinner, or any other fantasy.

The Closing

When all the gifts have been presented and received, the women gather for closing. The **Croning Woman** is brought to the center of the circle and all members connect by holding hands or placing hands gently on the woman in the center. They chant her name, give her hugs and kisses (if this is acceptable), pour love into her, wish her well with affirmations such as these:

May you walk with the Goddess.
May you be healthy.
May you be loved and loving and sexy all the rest of your days and nights!
May you have as much solitude and as much close-ness as you wish.
May you complete the tasks you have chosen.

The ritual ends with everyone participating in one of two chants by Shekhinah Mountainwater (see page 168).

Croning for Carol...

by Carol Laughing Water

148

Contributor Carol Laughing Water lives in Michigan. Spider Woman came to her in a dream and told her it was time for her Croning celebration. She honored her mother and older sister by accepting their Croning as part of her own. In a letter to the Spirit of Crone, Carol says:

> *I have feared you, Death Mother. You speak to me of grief, of pain. You ask much of me. I fear my heart will break, my mind snap. I am willing to let these parts of me go. And I am afraid. Teach me Your wisdom so that I can bring Your magic, Your mystery, into my world. Deep Raven Mother, turn me toward You, toward knowledge taught in the darkness of the moon. Let me feel You and respond to You as I meet You in my life each day. Help me see You as teacher, purifier, She-Who-Keeps-the-Fire-that-Burns-Away-All-Untruth. Take from me all that is unessential, that I may be real. Let me grow into You, Wise One, Earth Magician, Keeper of the Fire, Ancient Mother, Sacred One.*

The Invitation

You are welcome to camp for the weekend. Bring your own gear. Camping stoves will be needed. Bring sacred objects for ritual, drums, rattles, ritual garb. Let your instincts guide you! Any women who feel a readiness to ritualize the entrance into Cronehood are welcome to celebrate this rite of passage. Those of us making the transition will need the support of our sisters, pre-Crone and already Croned. All women of spirit are welcome!

In Cyprus, place of Aphrodite's temples and bath, on the February full moon, I had a lucid dream. Earlier I had been in Egypt touring the tombs. Perhaps it was the energy of the ancient places that led me to that dream, where I had lost the feminine mysteries. It was at that time that I knew I had entered the Crone stage of my life and needed a ritual. At the ritual, I would like (with the help of my friends) to act out the dream. Please consider taking part, and let me know. This dream is for all of us.

Rather than a preplanned ritual, I would ask that we consciously enter the ritual space and be response-able, allowing the ritual to become real and meaningful. Consider: Crone, Spider Woman, Black Madonna, witch, cauldron, healer, Wise Woman, death, Kali.

The Ritual

There was physical labor, creative energy, and decision-making. The gift of each woman had space to be received. I felt the weaving of the movement forward—I trusted the process. We passed the pipe in prayerful connection to all our relations. Body painted and death shield hung, I entered the womb of the Mother, supporting and supported by loving women. The spirits, grandmothers of this women's lodge, led us to wholeness as we claimed our own power, accepting the challenge of the heat, the letting go, the acceptance, the oneness, the gentle touch of loving hands, the caring for one another. I left the lodge in gratitude for all our relations and the stream of life that had made this reality.

On Saturday, we celebrated my Spider Woman dream by reenacting and ritualizing it, pulling dreamtime into this reality and then back again, claiming our selves, our lives, our connection with Spider Woman.

Saturday evening brought more women—and the mystical, magical time of ceremony—as by *luminiaro* light and smoke, we transformed ourselves through ancient rituals of foot bathing with magical healing herbs, massage with sacred oils and corn meal, anointing heads with oils of self-love and empowerment, touching each other deeply. We were in Women's Time. We celebrated skin, touch, massage, the senses. We enjoyed.

Each Crone claims her power by crossing the threshold, moving alone in her own style toward the doorway into the fullness of life and wisdom. We marked this passage. Each woman was received as newborn. We celebrated each other's willingness to risk, change, accept ourselves, be fully who we are. The drums rose and fell with the flow of the scene; the tempo was gentleness, love, tenderness, joy, wildness. I was moved to tears, remembering. My own mother was present, and my sister, and my chosen sisters; community moving as one for a moment in time, providing the "knowing" that this was feminine reality.

The gifts that I received are tools that will carry me through this Crone stage of my life: the Purple Hat (crown), the Red Bladed Knife, the Emerald Ring, the Crone Stole. There were many more gifts—works of art, treasures made and found—whose meanings for me will be revealed as time passes. At some point I became overwhelmed and encouraged myself to breathe into these gifts, knowing I would have the rest of my life to let in all this love and receiving. It slowly sank in that receiving is giving as well; there is no duality here. All enriches all in the circle of love energy.

More women arrived on Sunday. We were constantly circling, checking in, processing, working out the old, letting go, talking, sharing, laughing, telling stories, confronting the patriarchal within ourselves and others. The land was green, the weather held steady, clear. I walked the land, feeling the expansiveness of acres of wild open space. Feathers, deer tracks, the sighting of a doe or porcupine were treasured, respected as meaningful. Nature communicated. Time passed gently, without scarcity—limitless. I was healed of rushing, hurrying, being late or early. I am always "on time" when on the land.

The celebrating continued for days as women came and went. I felt the beauty of the enlarging circle as the women of the North met the women of the South and new bonds, new friendships, formed. We shared stories and saw that we are searching for the same basic things: love, community, a sense of comfort, abundance, security, being welcome, safe, at home. We saw that we were in need of healing.

We were born into and are imprinted by the wounding of patriarchy. We can heal and we must. We long for life in a feminine reality and we are willing to take the risks, make the changes necessary to have what we long for. We breathe, we drum, we circle, we talk, we scream, we move our bodies, we tell, we drum, we dance, we chant, we recover our wild, essential selves, our Maiden, our Mother, our Crone selves.

I thank you all for being a part of my journey, for following your own paths, for being who you are as fully as you can be moment to moment. Your lives touching mine bless me in ways I have no words to say or vision to know. It is not by chance we came together. I feel your strength, your recovery, your dreams for a life of freedom. I share those dreams. I welcome you into my heart and my life.

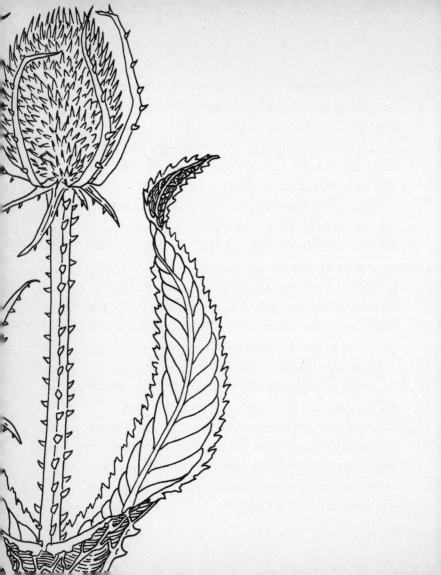

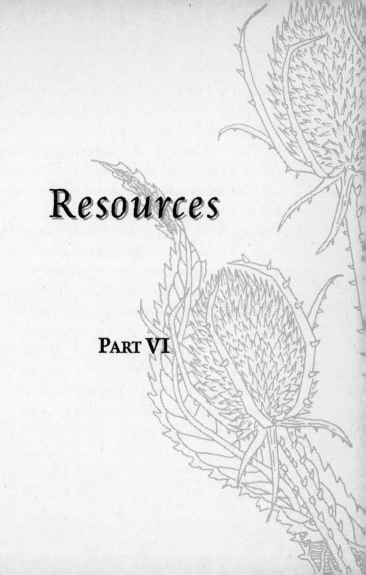

Resources

PART VI

Poetry and music are important parts of Croning, and this section provides both. Read for your satisfaction and enjoyment or use them in your own celebration. You may even want to write your own poetry or music. One of the wonderful parts of the life of a Crone is having enough experience that you can do almost anything and do it to your own specifications.

Another part of the *Resources* section (beginning on page 175) is devoted to guided meditations, which can be used for personal quiet healing sessions or as part of a larger ceremony. Read them aloud slowly into a tape recorder, being careful to take lengthy pauses, then play the meditations back in a quiet secluded spot.

Finally, a list of organizations on the national and regional level is included (beginning on page 185) to assist you in the event that you wish to seek membership in an established Croning group.

Crone Poetry and Music...

Crone . . . .
by Antiga[21]

Crone calls the darkness
> and then she takes you there
> shows you where you can dare
>> To be free
To feel what you cannot see
To be what you've been told
> you cannot be
Weird wild womoon—cunning cunt
> cutting away what nurtures you not
> undoing the knot
> unraveling, untying, unleashing, female fury

The Crone
> ha

> > ha

> > > ha

> > > > ha

> is not always kind
The Crone can drive you out of your mind
The Crone can unwind your sanity
Crone weighs it all in the scale of Maat
Crone tells you what to cut away
Crone will have her say

Crone calls the dying
    and sends them flying
    far into the unknown
    to rest their weary bones

Crone creeps up on you
    scares you half to death
Crone waits for your breath
    to disappear
Then she takes you with her
    into the darkness
    that is your own

Ancient One . . . .
by Antiga

Ancient one
    grandmother's grandmother's grandmother
Ancestress to many
    lets a womban know
That to honor an ancestress
    is to honor herself

Ancient one
Grey-haired one
    face furrowed deep from giving
    body bent low with living

carer for the young
protectress of the ones
                    who will carry on
bearer of tales of life and death

Ancient one
        turns the wheel
        keeps the cycle going
        cuts the cord when it's time to end
        releases spirit from body

Ancient one stands
        at the gateway of death
        welcoming those about to enter
        easing their passage to the center
        of the soul

Ancient one
        keeper of womban's wisdom
        helps a womban fly free
                    leaving behind
                    what she no longer needs
        helps a womban let go
                    of the grief that keeps her bound

Ancient one lets loose the sound
        of women who have found
                    themselves

Crowning Day, 1993 . . . .

by Lois H. Lockhart[22]

On this clear and sunny day in Saguaro National Park West
The Wise Women gather to crown three members as Crones.
Driving slowly, my daughter is looking for a narrow dusty trail,
When the bright table coverings appear through the brush.
Each woman is wearing a colorfully enhanced costume.
Inside a circle of stones, an altar is formed on a purple cloth,
Where offerings of food, flowers, trinkets, and photos are laid.
I contribute a velvet bag of stones, a bowl of pecans,
And my mother's picture taken when she was a young teacher.
Each woman adds a blessing and fuel to the symbolic fire.
Food prepared with love is spread for the celebration feast.

The excitement builds. I am about to be crowned a Crone!
How do I describe the feelings: The sacredness
And solemnity, the warmth of the women around me,
The reverence of being under the blue canopy,
Listening to desert birds. A soft breeze lifts the ribbons.
In silence, my daughter places the crown on my head.
Something changes within me, I feel regal, eloquent.
The Ancient Grandmothers whisper in my heart.
With thanks, I speak of my mother's strengths and
Her wisdom, hoping it has been bestowed upon me.

Floating around the table, I take nourishment.
Then clouds signal, time to leave this sacred ground.

Ravens catch the evening thermals, winging goodbye
From departed spirits. They call, share your knowledge,
Which we have done so through the years, now it is
A responsibility to proudly proclaim our age.
As Crowned Crones, we have an entrustment
From the Old Ones to command respect, be a force,
Use the hard-won wisdom, give in unusual forms,
Tell the world age is wonderful, glorious, heady,
And requires a new way of life.

Crone Unfolding . . . .
by Pat Watkins

Power is ours
With Wisdom to spare
Each line and deep furrow
And glowing grey hair

Attest to our lives
The laughter, the pain
In sunshine, in snowstorm
By lightning, by rain

We sing of creation, destruction,
Rebirth of friends
And of family
Of sweet mother earth

Sounds echo of magic
The universe brings
In circles and cycles
Old Autumns, young Springs

On this day in May
Our flesh and our bone
Stir fire and water
And wind and unknown

We raise high our spirits
Both ancient and bold
To celebrate age
Life's final unfold

The Croning . . . .
by Peggy Gilbert[23]

Lilac candles glow
like little crowns
in the darkening room
Outside the window
clouds shift and merge
over the silver Sound

As we eat and drink champagne
candles melt at their own pace

some short, some tall
like buildings in an old
neighborhood
or tombstones in Ireland
tilting toward each other
after centuries
of earth movement

Candles lean together
lavender wax mingling
like the talk around us:
talk of Elderhostel trips,
new dogs, pansies planted in pots,
radiation for beast cancer,
another grandchild on the way

The smell of lilacs
whispers to us
celebrating the cycle
of spring and restless
tombstones, molten wax
blending in the fire
of Crones claiming their
passion
          and power.

Ode to the Crone . . . .

by Joni Troutner

"I've come a long way baby"
is what I often hear
"I've come a long way maybe?"
rings also in my ear

So many new directions, roads,
trails, and paths to chart,
and now I come with renewed vows
to share life with a softer, lighter heart

Clear road maps, I often sidetrack,
when a new adventure pulls
Now I must continue forward,
as my growing future rules

Serenity is what I choose
to carry as my dream
The trail mix for the trip ahead
shooting upward on a beam

We gather on this desert land
to celebrate today
This golden age is a prism
on a shining brighter stage

To start this crowning journey,
a commitment I now choose
To grow in love, patience, tolerance,
for me, and you, and you

And when my final destination
to those future years release,
I hope a touch of magic grants me
a bit of wisdom and welcomed inner peace

Pillows . . . .

by Joan Weiss Hollenbeck

Seniors need pillows . . .
Pillows of comfort and rest
　　　　to ease body burdens
　　　　and smooth away
　　　　the wrinkles of the soul

Pillows of security
　　　　a safe, warm home,
　　　　the stuff called money,
　　　　and the ease it brings

Pillows of friendship
　　　　with kind men and women
　　　　to share joys and sadness

as a safety net
to soften the years

Pillows of art
    to nurture the spirit;
    good books and films,
    art and music
    to feed the senses

Pillows of laughter and faith
    fun in the sun and games
    to lift up the heart
    through nature and people
    to live in oneness

My View . . . .
by Ruth Gardner

Feeling age touch my shoulder,
I turned to see youth slipping by
I turned again to see age drawing ever closer
To see the fate that soon was mine

Awaiting a failing figure
I saw instead a vibrant Crone, frolicking and dancing,
Loving her wisdom sharing years
Finding joy instead of misery or tears

A Chant . . . .

by Shekhinah Mountainwater

168

I'm gonna live to a ripe old age
Write my books to the very last page
Keep all my teeth and eat real good
Have lots of friends in the neighborhood!

A Chant . . . .

by Shekhinah Mountainwater

I'm a prosperous, loving, healthy old Crone
With my cauldron and my cat and my cookin' stone
I'm a healer, I'm a lover, I'm together, I'm alone
I made it through the journey, now I'm safe at home!

I'm a crookedy, crotchety, cranky old Crone
'Cause your patriarchal ways cut me to the bone
I could curse you, I could hex you, I could turn you to stone
But I'm a harm-to-none witch, so just leave me alone!

How Could Anyone

©1998 Libby Roderick music

Woman Am I

170

Wo- man am I. Spi- rit am I. I am the

in- fi- nite with- in my soul. I

have no be- gin- ning and I have no end. I

have no be- gin- ning and I have no end. All this I am!

All this I am!

Traditional

Old Celtic Blessing

171

May the cir- cle be o- pen and ne-ver be un- bro-ken, may the love of the

God- dess be e- ver in your heart. Mer- ry meet, and mer- ry part, and

mer- ry meet a- gain!

Traditional

The Earth, the Air, the Fire, the Water

172

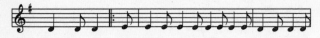

The earth, the air, the fire, the wa-ter, re-turn, re-turn, re-

turn, re-turn. Oh. Hey ye ye ye ye ye ye ye wo wo wo wo

River of Birds

There's a ri-ver of birds in mi-gra-tion, a

na-tion of wo-men with wings.

Traditional songs

My Mother's Song

Chorus (sing following each verse):

Wise Woman, Wise Woman, Wise Woman sitting here
Wise Woman, Wise Woman, Wise Woman here

Verse 1: Wise Woman, young woman, nestling me at her breast
Wise Woman, young woman, giving me her best

Verse 2: Wise Woman, growing woman, caring every way
Wise Woman, growing woman, showing me her way

Verse 3: Wise Woman, knowing woman, searching for a cure
Wise Woman, knowing woman, working to be pure

Verse 4: Wise Woman, Crone woman, knowing how far she's grown
Wise Woman, Crone woman, sharing what she's known

Verse 5: Wise Woman, aging woman, blessing all the strife
Wise Woman, aging woman, giving up her life

©1993 Renee Gardner

Ancient Mother

174

Chorus (African, traditional):

O la mama wa ha su kola
O la mama wa ha su wam
O la mama kow wey ha ha ha ha
O la mama ta te kayee

Traditional

Guided Meditation...

For guided meditation, you should find a very comfortable reclining place where your body is gently supported and you won't be disturbed. Then, close your eyes and listen. It is not important that you do anything—just listen. If your mind wanders off to other things, gently bring it back to the sound of your own voice, soothing and relaxing you. You may decide to write your own meditations as a means of getting a ceremony started or finished.

Meditation #1

Close your eyes and slowly take three very deep breaths. Finally, let the last breath all out and breathe at your normal pace, perhaps a little deeper and a little more slowly.

Imagine a large body of water. The temperature is perfect and as you kneel down and put your hand into the water; you are surprised at the feeling of delight it gives you. Standing, place one foot in the water. Be aware how safe and comfortable you are, how pleasant it is to have this water here just for you. There is no one about and you know there will be no one to disturb you. Know that you are perfectly safe. Walk out a little into the water and feel the gentle touch of the fluid moving up your body, cool and soothing. Lay back into the water and feel it supporting you fully. You know there is safety and delight in this water.

Lie quietly, bobbing a little and feeling the sun on your face, then feel yourself spreading out over the surface of the water. Imagine your body becoming one with the water as you spread further and further out over the surface. As you become the water, you can feel yourself flowing smoothly over the bottom, bumping softly against the shore and lapping lightly on the tree trunks that grow just next to the water. As you flow and move, feel how wonderful it is to be you, to be where you are and who you are. Know that you will always be safe and supported, flexible, and at peace. Be thankful for being who you are and what you are. Feel healthy and well, alive and in control of your life.

When you feel ready, gather yourself back into your body, float back to the shore, move your arms and legs a little, open your eyes and be back in the here and now.

Meditation #2

178

Imagine a cool forest of towering, elegant trees before you. Walking into the soft green grass, you see sparkles from the droplets of dew clinging to the grass and lower tree branches. Notice the beautifully colored wildflowers. You can see the lines of shadows from the trees scattered over the grass and smell a delicate fragrance wafting by you on the slight breeze.

Take a deep breath and feel yourself rising, weightless among the trees, above the flowers and the green grass. Look down and see the forest, small and green far below. You float along feeling at peace, cared for, loved and loving. Your body feels very heavy and yet you continue to float high above the green earth. You feel your body becoming larger and larger until you become the sky, the earth, and all that is on the earth. You are a part of all that is . . . you are all that is.

The peace is wonderful. Your energy feels infinite. Feel the seas and the land, all a part of you. Feel the creatures, the sun, and the moon, all a part of you. Feel yourself healing, creating, and loving. You are in perfect health, happy and peaceful, in charge of your life and your destiny. You know you are greater than you could have ever imagined when you entered the cool forest. You know a part of you will go on forever, loving, lovable, and loved. It is so peaceful.

Again take a deep breath and enjoy the oneness. Let it out slowly and feel the cosmos move with you. Enjoy and delight in this unbelievable place you have come to.

When you are ready to come back, move your hands, arms, feet, and legs, gently open your eyes, and be back in the here and now.

Meditation #3

Assume a comfortable position, close your eyes and take three very deep breaths. Let the last breath all out and breathe at your normal pace, perhaps a little deeper and a little more slowly.

In your mind's eye, see yourself walking outside, anyplace near where you are. Stand still and feel yourself expanding taller and wider until your vision is higher than the clouds. Look below you and see the earth, all of it swirling below you. You notice that your feet are no longer connected to the *earth. You are just floating far, far above it. You see the bright sun and feel the glorious feeling of just being free, unattached. As you float along you notice the sun is setting and it is beginning to get dark. The dark is wonderful, like soft, safe velvet and you feel at peace. Feel the pleasure at being in this quiet peaceful state. Then, gradually, you notice the sun rising. You feel serene and you have no responsibilities. All you have to do is just be.*

The sun rises overhead and then slowly starts its descent. You don't care one way or the other, if it rises or sets; it is just wonderful to exist. Relax into the stillness of your being and watch the sun begin to set again. You greet the night and its millions of stars, its tranquility, and feel again the pleasure of the dark. Acceptance is a wonderful feeling and you accept easily all that you are, can be, and ever will be. As you float along in the dark, you know that soon the sun will again rise, and that, too, will be as it should.

When it rises, you remind yourself of what you may have forgotten, that its power and glory are awesome and wonderful. Throughout the time of the sun, you glory in being alive, in being aware, and again, just in being. As time passes, so does the sun, and soon it begins its smooth departure. Eventually the many stars join you again and the peaceful night is upon you. You don't have to think. All you do is just enjoy and accept. And then, when the sun rises for the third time, look down at the earth, give thanks to All-That-Is for your place on earth and begin your descent.

Shortly you are back standing where you first stood when you started your expansion. Gently bring yourself back to the spot where you began the meditation, open your eyes, and be back in the here and now. Feel good about yourself, your journey and know that you are a wonderful, perfect human being, healthy and whole.

Meditation #4

Sit with your legs as close to you as possible. Pull yourself in tighter. Imagine you are a seed covered by an outer hull. Feel yourself quite small, and then notice that you have fallen into a polluted stream. You are drifting about on the surface but you are safe inside of your hull.

You can see the pollution all around you and you feel the water moving, throwing you about. You sink deeper into the messy, murky liquid and have no idea which way is up. You cannot see beyond your husk. You are powerless, vulnerable. You are tossed this way and that. There seems to be nothing you can do despite the fact that inside you are safe and pure.

Slowly you drift down, down, through the turbulent waters until you feel yourself on the very bottom. The waters still rage above you but suddenly you feel a tiny root protruding through your husk. It moves slowly and surely down through the bottom muck, deeper and deeper until it reaches bedrock far below. With a little twist the tiny root anchors itself to that stable, firm bedrock and you no longer are tossed and thrown. You feel the energy of Mother Earth rising through you.

Slowly you uncurl and send forth a shoot. The shoot rises straight and true guided by your inner wisdom. As it rises, it begins to clear the murk from the water. The water is still difficult to see through but it is getting lighter. The water around you becomes more and more clear until it is pure and clean. You continue to move up and, breaking through the water, you see the sun, the colors of the day, and you welcome the glorious world of blossoms all around you. Soon there are many of you above the rapidly changing, clearing water.

Beneath the bottom of the stream you feel your roots connecting with others like and different from you. It feels so connected, so one. And then you notice that you are connected above the surface of the water by fragrance, which you share and give each other. Feel the glory of being one, beneath and above. Feel the glory of sharing and caring, reclaiming the whole earth and sharing the whole earth.

Take a deep breath and enjoy being a part of this . . . of being this.

Organizations...

National Organizations

Crone Counsel

Contact Person: Constance Clover, Board President

E-mail: cbyram@adnc.com

Crone Counsel has a yearly fall gathering which is held in different cities in the western United States. There is no membership cost.

Council of Grandmothers

Contact Person: Judy O'Leary

Mail: P.O. Box 50512-85703, Tucson, AZ 85703

Telephone: (520) 792-6459

E-mail: GMCouncil@aol.com

Council of Grandmothers—an international, interracial, sacred circle of grandmothers over fifty—was formed in 1993 through the vision of the late Mary Diamond. Annual gatherings are held in natural settings and are based on a Native American prophecy: "When the grandmothers speak, the world will heal." Circles of women form to speak of their questions and knowledge, support each other, and honor the positive power and stability of elder women today. Celebrating their connection to their own divinity is done through music, dance, art, and ceremony. Encouragement is given for the formation of local ongoing grandmother circles and sharing wisdom with all generations.

This group has a yearly meeting at various locations. They encourage grandmothers in other places to start small support groups of grandmothers. They publish the Circle of Grandmothers *newsletter (see bibliography entry listed by newsletter editor Kit Wilson).*

International Council of Wise Women (a.k.a. International Council of Crones & Grandmothers)
Contact Person: Malka Golden-Wolfe
Internet: www.members.aol.com/iccghome
E-mail: ICCGhome@aol.com

ICW has chapters, a membership, and a newsletter. The organization states:

"The ICW is a wing of the Sedona Children's and Elders' Project, a nonprofit educational organization. Membership is open to women aged fifty and over and to younger women who wish to promote our goals and projects.

"Our purpose is to teach, empower, and encourage women to participate in the aging process with awareness, wisdom, and creativity. We recognize and celebrate the grandmother as respected elder, the Crone as wisdom carrier, the aging woman as guardian of the future. We honor ourselves and each other as we reclaim our place of respect in society.

"We consciously celebrate our coming of age and integrate the eldering process into our consciousness, enriching the

188

value of life for all generations. Learning to grow old creatively, we weave women's herstory, heritage, spirituality and culture in new ways. We are linking women from all parts of the planet to build a network of support and wisdom that will reverberate for eons into the future, leaving a legacy of respect and honor for every woman of age inspired by the Hopi prophecy: 'When the grandmothers speak, the earth will be healed.' We take the responsibility to be that voice."

Regional Organizations

Feminist Spiritual Community
Contact person: Debbie Leighton
Mail: HCR32, Box 227, Bath, ME, 04530

This group meets at the Friends Meeting House on Forest Avenue.

Desert Crones
Contact information: Check the Friday edition of the *Arizona Daily Star* for place and program

This group meets on the second Saturday of each month in Tucson, Arizona. The group's statement of purpose: "Desert Crones affirm the understanding of the aging process of women over fifty as we share, enlighten and celebrate our vibrant, fulfilling old womanhood."

Crone of Puget Sound

Contact Person: Peggy Gilbert
E-mail: Cronepg@worldnet.att.net

This Seattle group meets at one event monthly. The date varies. The group's statement of purpose: "Crone of Puget Sound is an organization that encourages and supports the personal unfolding and passage of its members from past outgrown roles and stereotypes into powerful, passionate, and satisfying old womanhood."

Meeting themes include membership, educational workshops, play days, potlucks, and picnics. Interest groups include Wellness, Conversation, Rolling Crones (singing), and others.

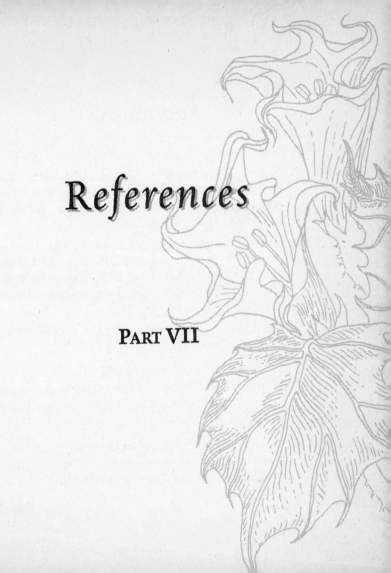

References

Part VII

Footnotes

1. Quoted from Jean Shinoda Bolen's *Crossing to Avalon* (San Francisco: HarperCollins, 1994), pages 98–99.

2. Historically, the Greeks and Romans showed the presence of strong patriarchal influence unlike the earlier, more peaceful, civilizations. Thus, their goddesses could be vengeful and warlike.

3. Much of the goddess history and information in this chapter is paraphrased from Patricia Monaghan's book, *The New Book of Goddesses & Heroines* (St. Paul, MN: Llewellyn Publications). It appears here with her consent.

4. Malka Golden-Wolfe wrote this piece specifically for *Celebrating the Crone*.

5. Traditional Native American chant.

6. Excerpted from *The Grandmother of Time* by Zsuzsanna Budapest (San Francisco: Harper & Rowe), page 198.

7. Traditional song.

8. Renee Gardner wrote "My Mother's Song" in 1993. Renee lives in Washington with her husband and their two children. She is a Crone In Training (CIT).

9. Traditional song.

10. All underlined passages in this ritual are reprinted with permission from Marcia Starck's *Women's Medicine Ways* (Freedom, CA: The Crossing Press, 1993).

11. Any significant nurturing relationship can be referred to here.

12. Traditional song.

13. Traditional song.

14. Reprinted from "Transformation of Our Lives" in issue 14 of *Woman of Power* magazine, pages 14–15. The original text noted fifty-six as the age at which Croning occurs. The author has changed that number to "between the ages of fifty-six and fifty-eight" for purposes of greater accuracy.

15. All underlined passages in this ritual are reprinted with permission from Meridel Le Sueur's *Winter Prairie Woman* (Minneapolis, MN: Midwest Villages Publishers, 1990).

16. Reprinted with permission from Susun S. Weed's *Menopausal Years: The Wise Woman Way* (Woodstock, NY: Ash Tree Publishers, 1992), pages 124–125.

17. Traditional song.

18. Weed, *Menopausal Years,* op. cit.

19. "How Could Anyone," © 1988 Libby Roderick Music, from the recording *If You See a Dream* (Anchorage, AK: Turtle Island Records), is reprinted with permission.

20. To contact Shekhinah Mountainwater or to arrange for appearances, write to her at P.O. Box 2991, Santa Cruz, CA, 95063.

21. Antiga is a feminist, witch, writer, artist, and outrageous woman. She turned sixty-seven in 1999 and "finds these years challenging, exciting, and scary yet."

22. Lois is a pagan Crone and a member of Desert Crones (page 188). She's a Master Gardener, Master Composter, and a member of Tucson Organic Gardeners. Lois is also a poet, wife, mother, and grandmother.

23. Peggy is a retired college English teacher living in Washington. She is co-editor of *The Crone Connection* (a quarterly newsletter of the Crone of Puget Sound organization—see page 189) and the author of *A Time to Dance* (if you're interested in Peggy's work, please look for her book in the collection of your local library; it is unfortunately out of print at this time and unavailable for commercial purchase). This poem was originally published in *The Crone Connection*.

Annotated Bibliography

Printed Matter

Beck, Renee and Sidney Barbara Metrick. *The Art of Ritual.* Berkeley, CA: Celestial Arts, 1990.

Bolen, Jean Shinoda. *Crossing to Avalon: A Woman's Midlife Pilgrimage.* San Francisco, CA: HarperCollins, 1994.

Bolen takes us on her midlife-crisis journey through the landscapes of Chartres, Glastonbury, the fictional Avalon, the inner dark forest, the wasteland (and its greening at Findhorn), and the islands of Iona and Lindisfarne to obtain the Grail, a feminine symbol of women's way of knowing with the body and living this knowing. It is, as she says, a "personal and planetary story."

Bozarth, Barkley and Hawthorne. *Stars in Your Bones: Emerging Signposts on our Spiritual Journeys.* St. Cloud, MN: North Star Press, 1990.

Dr. Bozarth explores the Goddess, the androgynous nature of Christ and the Christian concept of God, women's relationships with each other and with men, all in concert with the beautiful, sometimes ethereal art of Julia Barkley

Budapest, Zsuzsanna. *Grandmother of Time*. San Francisco, CA: HarperCollins, 1989.

196
For both beginners and experienced practitioners: New approaches to today's rituals, from birthdays and dedications of newborn babies to purifying our homes and protecting us in travel. Web site: www.netwiz.net/ZBudapest/ Telephone: 1-900-737-4637

Cameron, Ann. *Daughters of Copper Woman*. Vancouver, BC: Press Gang Publishers, 1981.

Cameron weaves life's myths and images together using fictional characters in an eventful saga demonstrating how to endure and survive. A marvelous spiritual, fiction, nonfiction example for women everywhere.

Conway, D. J. *Maiden, Mother, Crone*. St. Paul, MN: Llewellyn Publications, 1995.

Presents goddess myths that will illuminate understanding of ancient, universal human challenges that still exist today. Offers in-depth explanations of goddess archetypes and their relevance to twentieth century living.

Duerk, Judith. *Circle of Stones: Woman's Journey To Herself*. San Diego, CA: Luramedia, 1989.

The central axis around which this book evolves is that woman's spirit-self is found in solitude, in recognizing the

*validity and truth of her own feeling values and that one's
personhood is not found in safe conformity to outer values
but in the darkness of personal discovery.*

Eiker, Diane and Sapphire, eds. *Keep Simple Ceremonies.*
Portland, ME: Astarte Shell Press, 1995.

*Compendium of ceremonies for seasons of women's lives
and seasons of the earth. Music, chants, history, and much
more, arranged in a very understandable, beautiful, illustrated work.*

Eisler, Riane. *Chalice and the Blade.* Cambridge, MA:
Harper and Rowe, 1987.

*In this book, Eisler finds a prototype for our future from the
ruins of agrarian villages of the Neolithic era. Calling on the
scholarship of anthropologist Marija Gilmbutas and others,
she maintains that those societies were egalitarian, cooperative and peace-loving rather than dominating, competitive,
and warlike. She bids us to emulate them and offers ways to
transform our world into a place free from the exploitation
of the earth, its peoples, and all its creatures.*

Estes, Clarissa Pinkola. *Women Who Run With Wolves.* New
York: Ballantine Books, 1992.

*Estes deepens and expands stories and myths from the past
that we might recognize a powerful psychological force*

within us. This is a collection of traditional stories with fem-
inist interpretations—enlightening and empowering for
every woman in search of her own inner spirit.

Gimbutas, Marija. *The Goddesses and Gods of Old Europe:*
Myths and Cult Images. Berkeley, CA: University of
California Press, 1982.

Gimbutas writes of European civilization between 6500 and
3500 B.C. before Greek or Judeo-Christian civilizations
flourished. The book is very well illustrated with pho-
tographs of ancient sculptures and artifacts.

Jacobs, Ruth Harriet. *Be An Outrageous Older Woman.*
Manchester, CT: Knowledge, Ideas, & Trends, 1993.

Hopes, hints, blueprints, warmth, and poetry for old
women, puncturing many myths of aging. Bibliographical
references and index are included.

Krielkamp, Anne. *Crone Chronicles: A Journal of Conscious*
Aging. P.O. Box 81-WP, Kelly, WY, 83011 (or visit the
internet: www.cronechronicles.com/index.html).

Publisher and editor Anne Krielkamp guides this superb
magazine's exploration of Cronedom in ways appealing to
those interested in aging consciously and fully. Crones write
of Cronings, of loves and disappointments, remembrances as
mothers and daughters, and hopes for the future. Krielkamp

publishes the truth in colorful art, poetry and short stories. This totally readable magazine was started in 1989.

Le Sueur, Meridel. *Winter Prairie Woman*. Minneapolis, MN: Midwest Villages Publishers, 1990.

Marks, Kate, ed. *Circle of Song: Songs, Chants and Dance for Ritual and Celebration*. Amherst, MA: Full Circle Press, 1995.

Three hundred Native American, African, Celtic, Mayan, Maori, Aboriginal, and Japanese songs and chants from ancient to modern. Words and music are included for most of the songs.

Monaghan, Patricia. *The New Book of Goddesses and Heroines*. St. Paul, MN: Llewellyn Publications, 1998.

A profound encyclopedia with clear, beautifully written, information about the Goddesses. Each Goddess has her stories and her realms intelligibly defined and explained.

Mountainwater, Shekhinah. *Ariadne's Thread: A Workbook of Goddess Magic*. Freedom, CA: Crossing Press, 1991.

Roderick, Libby. "How Could Anyone," from the recording *If You See a Dream*, Turtle Island Records, 1988.

Libby also has a book (When I Hear Music), CD, and cassette available from Turtle Island. Write to Turtle Island Records, P. O. Box 203294, Anchorage, AK, 99520-3294.

Rupp, Joyce. *The Star in My Heart: Experiencing Sophia, Inner Wisdom.* San Diego, CA: Luramedia, 1990.

Joyce Rupp connects with Sophia, the feminine wisdom in her own wisdom writing about Sophia's presence in her life.

Starck, Marcia. *Women's Medicine Ways.* Freedom, CA: The Crossing Press, 1993.

Various cultural traditions are presented. Ceremonies from the distant past with explanations to inspire us to create those ceremonies again, to honor times of our lives.

Walker, Barbara G. *The Crone: Woman of Age, Wisdom and Power.* San Francisco, CA: HarperCollins, 1988.

In this spiritually satisfying book, Walker writes about the repression, denial, and punishment of wisdom among old women. She encourages women to say no to patriarchal power and to learn by remembering our collective history.

———. *Women's Rituals.* San Francisco, CA: HarperCollins, 1990.

The author offers techniques, procedures, and suggestions for individual or group rituals for women seeking a broadened spiritual experience. She presents traditional religion alternatives to those questing for the feminine spirit in themselves and each other.

———. *The Women's Encyclopedia of Myths and Secrets.*
Edison, NJ: Castle Books, 1983.

*A resource on women's history, this twelve-hundred-page
book carefully describes, defines and explains myth figures
and happenings from Abaddon to Zurvan. Included are
many photographs. Entries demonstrate the dominant role
women have played in the evolution of our culture.*

Ward, Edna. *Celebrating Ourselves: A Crone Ritual Book.*
Portland, ME: Astarte Shell Press, 1992.

*Edna Ward describes the Croning Ceremony of the Feminist
Spiritual Community of Portland, Maine. In addition to the
ritual, the book includes further resources for exploring
aging, ageism, and the lives of old women.*

Weed, Susun. *Menopausal Years: The Wise Woman Way.*
Woodstock, NY: Ash Tree Publishing, 1992.

*Weed writes wisely of changes women make as they experi-
ence menopause. She recommends natural healing remedies
from herbs to meditation to avoid osteoporosis and quickly
relieve hot flashes. She guides women in ways of remaining
active, healthy, and satisfied in this stage of their lives.*

Wilson, Kit, ed. *Circle of Grandmothers.* Tucson, AZ:
Council of Grandmothers.

*This newsletter is put out by Council of Grandmothers (see
their listing in organizations).*

Video

Pearson, Carol Lynn. "Mother Wove the Morning." Walnut Creek, WA: Carol Lynn Pearson, 1992.

Sixteen women throughout history search for God the Mother and invite her back into the human family. A one-woman play.

Sedona Children's and Elder's Project. "Crone Counsel III: Celebrating Our Lives." Sedona, AZ: International Council of Crones and Grandmothers.

Documentary of conference of over three hundred Crones with stories, speakers and activities.

Spittler, Connie, producer/director. "Wise Women Video Series." Tucson, AZ: ConText Productions, 1994.

"Celebration of Age: The Croning Ceremony." Explores contemporary adaptations of ancient custom of Croning. Using music, story, and symbol, inspired older women honor this stage of life.

"Architects of Change: Two Grandmothers." Earth dome and straw bale homes by off-the-grid grandmothers.

"Grandmothers Speak: Healing the Earth." Sixteen women of age gather together in the desert, seeking new answers to old questions.

"Sage for All Seasons." *Features seventy-year-old Shirley Tassencourt, sculptor, philosopher, environmentalist, poet, builder of earth dome houses in the desert.*

Wilson, David, producer and Cynthia Scott, director. "Company of Strangers." Ottowa, Ontario: National Film Board of Canada, 1990.

Several women leave by bus for a day's outing. The day extends to several as the travelers search for and share their almost forgotten survival skills.

203

Index

crown, 2, 37, 41–42, 58, 71, 78, 84–85, 94, 100, 105, 116, 121, 127, 138, 143, 152, 161–163, 166

crystals, 98, 134

cycle(s), 40, 89, 110, 160, 163–164

dancing, 47, 76, 80, 88–92, 96, 104, 117, 127, 153, 167, 186

darkness, 30, 32, 40, 44, 76–77, 108, 110, 138–139, 148, 158–159, 180

daughter(s), 4, 13, 29, 47, 57–58, 60, 71–72, 74, 91, 121, 130, 161

death, 10, 31–32, 40, 54, 56, 69–70, 76–79, 84, 89, 91, 93, 106–110, 114–115, 117, 148, 150, 159–160

Decades, 46, 120, 135

depression, 13, 44, 59, 117

Desert Crones, 12, 87–88, 130, 188

drum(s), 12, 47, 61, 68–69, 72, 96, 114, 122, 134, 149, 151, 153

elder(s), 2–3, 16, 20–21, 36, 39, 49, 56, 72, 95, 131, 134–135, 140–141, 143–144, 164, 186–187

experience (see also maturity), 2–3, 5–8, 10, 14, 18, 21, 37, 39, 48–49, 52, 54, 57–58, 60, 68–69, 72, 81, 84, 94–95, 111, 125, 135, 145, 156

equinox, 124

family, 15–17, 37, 79, 104, 131, 162

fear, 10, 13, 25, 44, 69, 78–79, 109–110, 148

feminine, 2, 4, 19, 24–26, 36–37, 42, 44, 58, 61, 81, 95, 121–122, 149, 151, 153, 158, 188

feasting, 47, 72, 96, 122, 127, 134, 161

formal, 8, 36–37, 42, 46, 52, 56, 60, 64, 94, 106

friendship, 11, 13–15, 20, 37, 54–55, 59, 74, 80, 103–104,

REACH FOR THE MOON

Llewellyn publishes hundreds of books on your favorite subjects! To get these exciting books, including the ones on the following pages, check your local bookstore or order them directly from Llewellyn.

ORDER BY PHONE

- Call toll-free within the U.S. and Canada, 1-800-THE-MOON
- In Minnesota, call (651) 291-1970
- We accept VISA, MasterCard, and American Express

ORDER BY MAIL

- Send the full price of your order (MN residents add 7% sales tax) in U.S. funds, plus postage & handling to:

  Llewellyn Worldwide
  P.O. Box 64383, Dept. K292-5
  St. Paul, MN 55164–0383, U.S.A.

POSTAGE & HANDLING

(For the U.S., Canada, and Mexico)

- $4.00 for orders $15.00 and under
- $5.00 for orders over $15.00
- No charge for orders over $100.00

International orders: Airmail—add freight equal to price of each book to the total price of order, plus $5.00 for each non-book item (audio tapes, etc.).

Surface mail—Add $1.00 per item.

We ship UPS in the continental United States. We ship standard mail to P.O. boxes. Orders shipped to Alaska, Hawaii, The Virgin Islands, and Puerto Rico are sent first-class mail. Orders shipped to Canada and Mexico are sent surface mail.

Allow 2 weeks for delivery on all orders. Postage and handling rates subject to change.

DISCOUNTS

We offer a 20% discount to group leaders or agents. You must order a minimum of 5 copies of the same book to get our special quantity price.

FREE CATALOG

Get a free copy of our color catalog, *New Worlds of Mind and Spirit.* Subscribe for just $10.00 in the United States and Canada ($30.00 overseas, airmail). Many bookstores carry *New Worlds*—ask for it!

Visit www.llewellyn.com for more information.

Instant Handwriting Analysis:
A Key to Personal Success

by Ruth Gardner

For those who wish to increase self-awareness, graphology is a key to success. With practice, one can make graphology an objective method for opening and giving feedback to the inner self. Author Ruth Gardner makes the process quick and easy, illustrating how letters are broken down vertically into three distinctive zones that help you explore your higher philosophies, daily activities and primal drives. She also explains how the size, slant, connecting strokes, spacing, and amount of pressure are interpreted. Also included are sections on doodles and social graphology.

Instant Handwriting Analysis provides information for anyone interested in pursuing graphology as a hobby or career. It includes listed resources such as national graphology organizations and several correspondence schools.

0-87542-251-9, 7 x 10, 159 PP., ILLUS. $15.95

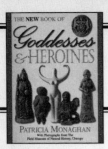

**The New Book of
Goddesses & Heroines**

by Patricia Monaghan

The third edition of this classic reference offers a complete, shining collection of goddess myths from around the globe. Discover more than 1,500 goddesses in Australia, Africa, North and South America, Asia, and Europe. This new edition also adds hundreds of new entries to the original text—information found only in rare or limited editions and obscure sources.

There is a new section, "Cultures of the Goddess," which provides the location, time and general features of the major religious system detailed in the myths. A comprehensive index, "Names of the Goddess," provides all available names, with variants. Stories, rites, invocations, and prayers are recorded in the "Myths" section, as well as a list of common symbols. Never before has such a vast panorama of female divinity been recorded in one source.

1-56718-465-0, 8½ x 11, 384 PP., ILLUS. $19.95

In Praise of the Crone: A Celebration of Feminine Maturity

by Dorothy Morrison

When Dorothy Morrison began her menopausal metamorphosis at the early age of 32, she thought her life was over. Then she discovered a reason to celebrate: she'd been invited to the Crone's party! Meet your hostess and mentor, your Personal Crone. Mingle a bit and find your Spirit Self. Discover why the three of you belong together. Learn to balance yourself, gather wisdom, reclaim your life, and make the most of your natural beauty. Then meander into the Crone's kitchen and find home remedies that can take the edge off minor menopausal aggravations without the use of hormone replacement therapy or prescription drugs.

Written with humor and compassion from someone who's been there, *In Praise of the Crone* alleviates the negativity and fear surrounding menopause with a wealth of meditations, invocations, rituals, spells, chants, songs, recipes and other tips that will help you successfully face your own emotional and spiritual challenges.

1-56718-468-5, 6 x 9, 288 pp. $14.95

Congratulations

CRONE
_____

You are granted Cronehood in honor of your experience, age, and wisdom.

From this day forward, you are entitled to sign yourself:

CERTIFIED CRONE (C.C.)

DATE
_____

SISTERHOOD OF CRONES

Congratulations!

Because Croning is a serious and wonderful ritual and because it usually ends with singing, merriment, and dancing, it seems appropriate that the new Crone receive a tangible symbol of her achievement. This bound-in certificate (see reverse side) may be appropriate as a finishing touch to the ceremony, serving as both a valuable symbol of the Croning ritual and a constant reminder of the initiate's newly affirmed status as an elder. It is designed to fit a 3"x5" photo frame and is intended for display by the initiated Crone.

Tear along the perforated edge and place in 3"x5" photo frame for display.